THE SILHOUETTE SOLUTION

"Brenda's capsule wardrobe system is a lifesaver . . . I will never look at my clothes the same way again!"

—**Fran Drescher,**
star of *The Nanny*

The Silhouette Solution

BRENDA COOPER

Using What You Have to
Get the Look You Want

Illustrations by Jessica Durrant

CLARKSON POTTER/PUBLISHERS
NEW YORK

I dedicate this book to YOU

May you discover, accept, and
celebrate your authentic self,
which is always in style!

CONTENTS

FOREWORD BY FRAN DRESCHER / 9

INTRODUCTION / 13

RESOURCES / 248

ACKNOWLEDGMENTS / 254

PART ONE

YOUR INNER CLOSET

1
because you're worth it!

18

2
candid closet conversations

36

PART TWO

THE SILHOUETTE SOLUTION

3
terrific tops & beautiful bottoms

52

4
stepping out in style

86

5
combining
your
silhouettes
104

6
personality
pieces
120

7
dressing
for the
nine-to-five
146

8
dressing
for a
casual vibe
170

9
dressing
for special
occasions
184

PART THREE

IT'S TRANS-
FORMATION
TIME

10
shopping
your own
closet
210

11
set yourself
up for
success
228

12
your time
to shine
242

FOREWORD

Dear reader,

I applaud you for picking up this book! Now you will know, as I do, the genius that is Brenda Cooper. I've had the pleasure and delight of working with Brenda for more than three decades, and the great privilege of calling her a friend.

Brenda and I met on the set of a short-lived CBS series, *Princesses,* which I starred in alongside my friend and fashion icon Twiggy. Brenda served as the assistant costume designer for the show, and, from our very first fitting, she completely changed how I thought about fashion. Brenda taught me that looking fabulous starts on the inside, and she helped me to feel more comfortable in my own skin. With her passion for fashion and her relationships with the people underneath the clothes, I knew she *had* to be the designer for my next series, which ended up being *The Nanny*.

Brenda's vision for *The Nanny* was genius. She took what could have conceivably been a pretty boring sartorial layout and made it instantly iconic using her endless creativity, love of clothes, and unique ability to combine style and wit in service of elevating comedy. Needless to say, the costumes on *The Nanny* quickly became as big a star as the character of Fran Fine herself! Not surprisingly, Brenda won a well-deserved Emmy for her work on the show—the only one the show received, despite numerous nominations across multiple categories. To this day, there is ne'er an interview about the show—be it on television, in magazines, or online—that doesn't discuss the "look" and style of *The Nanny* and its impact on the 1990s and today.

Despite a limited budget during the first couple of years of the show, Brenda always reassured me she would be able to come up with fantastic options: "Fran, *darling*, you don't need to spend a lot of money to have great style. You just have to choose the right pieces!" The right pieces became a turtleneck, a pencil skirt, tights, and high-heeled suede pumps that Brenda would creatively transform into many different looks.

By using this book, you now have the opportunity to benefit from the same timeless principles that Brenda came up with on the set of *The Nanny* all those years ago! In the following pages, Brenda will show you how to take a limited amount of clothing—four tops, four bottoms, and eight pairs of shoes—and transform them into a complete wardrobe! Brenda's capsule wardrobe system is a lifesaver for every woman who has struggled to be inventive with the clothes in her closet. I can't tell you how Brenda's style genius has liberated me. I will never look at my clothes the same way again!

Most important, *The Silhouette Solution* will encourage you to love the body you have rather than the body you think you *should* have. Years ago, when I was first starting my career as an actress, I was constantly told by others—managers, casting executives, the media—how I *should* look. Brenda was my guiding light for many of my years in showbiz, constantly reassuring me that I looked *fabulous* and helping me to make it so. If nothing else, my wish is for you to experience a new kind of confidence that I believe you can only get when you know you look great. I guarantee that, by the end of this book, you will be delighted and inspired to step into your best self!

With love,

Fran

Brenda's style genius has liberated me. I will never look at the clothes in my closet in quite the same way again!

"Fashion isn't always in style, but style is always in fashion."

INTRODUCTION

The Silhouette Solution was born out of necessity. When I landed the job as head costume designer and stylist for *The Nanny* in 1993, it became my responsibility to create the entire look of the show. This meant I had to come up with 40 to 50 outfits every week for the lead, Fran Drescher, as well as for all the supporting actors and guest stars. Delighted as I was to be a part of this fantastic series, there were many challenges. We had an extremely slim budget (to put it mildly), as the show was not yet a proven success. Our production schedule seemed to move at the speed of light, allowing only three and a half days each week to shop the whole of Los Angeles and New York in search of the right clothes for each character. Once I had the appropriate pieces, every item had to be refitted perfectly for each personality and body type, coordinated into complete outfits, and often redesigned and embellished for each cast member.

I had to figure out a way to create an endless variety of stylish, fun, and distinct outfits that took minimal time to put together and could be done on the cheap. To find the solution, I looked to my past. As a young girl growing up in England, I was captivated by the movies I watched with my mother on Sunday afternoons. It was the simple, sleek, and unique stylings of Academy Award–winning costume designer Edith Head that caught my attention in particular. The stars she dressed always looked timeless and elegant, whether they were wearing a nightgown or an evening gown.

Inspired by this chic simplicity, I set out to strategically gather a group of garments that I knew from experience were timeless and universally flattering: four terrific tops, four beautiful bottoms, four flat shoes, and four heels. These practical and complimentary pieces form the basic canvas for dozens of outfits that can be repurposed and accessorized to ultimately make each woman look completely original. Actors I worked with were thrilled to avoid the exhaustive hours of trying on endless racks of clothes to find the right look. Shape and fit were no longer an issue

Your attire is your most public form of self-expression. What you wear shows others who you are, how you feel, and the person you aspire to be.

because of the adaptability of the pieces from one body type to another. Fittings became fun, quick, and creative, and actors always came away from the experience feeling beautiful, confident, and excited about what they were wearing, instead of stressed, uncomfortable, and self-conscious.

This is the way getting dressed every day should be.

Clothes have always been a source of inspiration, delight, and curiosity for me, as far back as I can remember, and I want every woman to feel this same joy when getting ready for her day. While many consider the daily task of getting dressed a rather superficial pursuit, I've come to realize that fashion and style involve your inner emotions as much as your outer appearance.

Your attire is your most public form of self-expression. What you wear shows others who you are, how you feel, and the person you aspire to be. Dressing can and should be so much more than just covering your body; it is a powerful form of self-care. The majority of my clients feel a greater sense of well-being when they know they are dressed in an attractive outfit that fits and flatters their bodies. But with the world of fashion continually bombarding women with pressure to keep up with the latest trends and buy new items every season, it can often feel overwhelming to navigate our closets, pull together a great outfit, and present our most authentic selves to the world.

In the following pages, I will guide you through the same journey I take my clients on every day. Our destination? A place where:

- You look better than you ever imagined possible in a fraction of the time.

- Dressing is easy, quick, and creative.

- You feel authentic and confident in your own skin.

By the end of this book, you'll have the tools to dress in a way that flatters your body, your lifestyle, and your personality, regardless of your size or shape. You will learn how to create a versatile wardrobe of fabulously functional clothes that you absolutely love. You will experience the joy and freedom that comes with letting go of all the items that no longer serve you. You will be able to easily compose fresh, stylish outfits in less time (and with less stress!) on any budget, leaving you free to focus on what's most important to you, whatever that might be.

When you look in the mirror each morning, you will see an attractive, self-assured, and satisfied woman. When dressing becomes an opportunity for celebration instead of a source of confusion, you create the conditions necessary for your own success, fulfillment, and happiness every day.

When we feel great and comfortable in our own skin, it's hard to stop us. Ready to get going?

The Silhouette Solution is foolproof, budget-proof, economy-proof, trend-proof, and even disaster-proof. Whether you work from home or commute to an office, whether you love or loathe wearing heels, the Solution is not about buying the exact items in this book; it's flexible, and it can be tailored to your taste and lifestyle. It's about simplifying your relationship to your closet. In fact, it helped me to know *exactly* what to pack when I looked out the window of my Los Angeles home, saw a bright orange sky—a wildfire in the distance—and had to hop in the car and maybe never return to my possessions. Luckily, the fire never reached my neighborhood, but when someone asks me what clothes I would grab if my home were burning, I can answer with confidence, *The Silhouette Solution, darling!*

Part
one

Your Inner Closet

To be yourself in a world that is
constantly trying to make you
something else is the greatest
accomplishment.

—RALPH WALDO EMERSON

because you're
worth it!

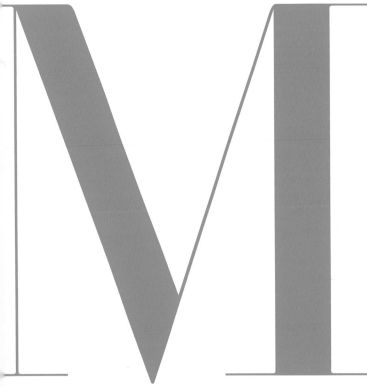

MOST PEOPLE THINK dressing begins when you open your closet, but nothing could be further from the truth. It actually begins as soon as you start thinking about what to wear.

You probably start by thinking about what kind of day you are preparing for, how you want to look, and even how you want to feel. You may be dressing for work, to exercise, for a first date, or even for a special event. While dressing is a powerful form of self-expression, the negative feelings around how you look or how your clothes fit can ignite low-grade anxiety, increase self-doubt, and decrease your confidence level, all before you've even opened your closet door.

It doesn't seem to matter whether you are short, tall, plus-size, or slim—most women have negative thoughts about their bodies. In fact, a survey by *Glamour* magazine found that 97 percent of women have negative thoughts about their appearance, and Refinery29 similarly reported that only 20 percent of women are completely happy with their bodies and their weight.

We all struggle with body acceptance in one way or another. In my case, my negative thinking has always been focused on my legs. From an early age, I decided that my legs *should* look different from the way they do. They should be longer. My calves should be smaller. My ankles should be thinner. But they are not. They are the way they are. And I get to choose whether to make peace with the body I have, with grace and gratitude, or be miserable comparing myself to others. Over the years, I've chosen to make peace with my body. When I look in the mirror now, I like and appreciate what I see.

I want you to experience that same joy and freedom when you look in the mirror. And I believe you absolutely can! I want you to celebrate and accept your shape and size without comparing yourself to others. I want you to not only love who you are, but also how you look.

When I style women (yes, even celebrities), the first thing I address, before we start talking about clothing, is their self-image. I ask them one simple question: What do you *like* about your body and appearance? There is often a pause or a momentary look of panic, and then, with more than a little hesitation, ladies will list off their perceived physical flaws first. I've heard complaints ranging from a flabby stomach, large hips, and small boobs to generally wanting to be thinner or taller. Disempowering beliefs, judgments, and conclusions are quick to roll off our tongues, but our positive attributes and strengths are often harder for us to identify and embrace.

For that reason, our journey to a fabulously functional wardrobe will not begin in your physical closet, but, rather, in what I call your "inner closet." It resides in that small space between your ears that's typically filled to bursting with negative self-talk, critical opinions, and disapproving thoughts about yourself and your body.

It's this little den of disempowerment that can subconsciously sabotage your life. For me, it has never been enough to just make a woman look magnificent on the outside. That part is easy. As a professional stylist, I am committed to helping women *feel* as good about themselves on the inside as I know I can make them look on the outside. In order to reveal the confident, empowered, fabulous woman I know you are, creating a positive and more accepting relationship between the inner closet of your mind and your outer closet is an essential "must-do."

Not sure what I'm talking about? Let me take you on a journey to your past.

Think of a time when you dressed up for a special evening or event, expecting to feel like a million dollars, but instead you spent most of the night fiddling with an ill-fitting garment or sitting down to relieve your aching feet.

Here's a news flash: We can't blame the clothes. Or the shoes. We chose those items. The voice of our inner closet convinced us to buy the latest trend so we'd feel hip and modern, the shapewear so we'd feel slimmer, and the high-heeled shoes so we would feel tall and sexy. But, surprise! We didn't. The trendy clothes made us feel uncomfortable; the shapewear left us suffocating; the shoes spent most of the evening furtively slipped off under the table, effectively chaining us to our chair and killing our chance of having an unforgettable time. But it doesn't have to be that way.

If you find that your negative inner voice has misled you for years, I'd be willing to bet that, as a result, you have a closet full of clothes that aren't right for you.

Want to know how I know? According to the *Wall Street Journal*, the average consumer wears 20 percent of her clothes 80 percent of the time. That means that the other 80 percent of the clothes spend their time just hanging there unused and sometimes never worn. The cause? That darned inner closet. We drop the credit card to feel better about ourselves, because our inner closet's critic is telling us that *more* is the solution. We buy more clothes instead of buying the right pieces, and we continually bring home items that don't really fit or flatter us. No wonder we never feel truly comfortable or secure in our own skin. You may be one of the very small minority of women who stand loud and proud in your shoes each day, but for the 97 percent of us who admit to having a negative body image and would like to change it, we've got some work to do.

so where *do* our negative beliefs come from?

To get to the bottom of our disempowering thoughts and beliefs, we have to understand where they come from. The media often sets ridiculously unattainable standards of physical beauty for women. In fact, 98 percent of the advertisements we see on a daily basis are digitally enhanced, creating a brighter, smoother, slimmer, and allegedly more charismatic version of the original model. Even the models and celebrities promoting these products wish they looked like their digitally enhanced images! We are conditioned to believe that we *should* look different from the way we do. We pick on and deride ourselves for not being able to live up to this idealized standard of beauty instead of celebrating and illuminating our natural assets. We abandon our authentic selves in pursuit of these impossible and inauthentic standards, often playing into the very hands of the advertisers who are trying to sell us their "solution."

We go on crazy fad diets, overexercise, and fill our wardrobes with the kinds of clothes that do not sustain long-term confidence or joy. So why do we chase these insanely unattainable, often biologically impossible standards? We think that if we look a certain way or achieve this unrealistic ideal of beauty, we will feel more included and more loved by others, like ourselves more, and obtain our ultimate goal: happiness. Sadly, the opposite so often happens. For all their efforts, many women end up feeling depressed, anxious, and ashamed.

family
& childhood

It's not just the media that has contributed to our beliefs about our bodies. For many of my clients, their childhood experiences have negatively impacted how they view their own appearance as adults. Those past experiences are alive today, stored as negative thoughts taking up valuable space in their inner closets. They are still affected by judgments that people directed at them when they were younger.

It's those negative inner voices that influence not only how we dress but how we view ourselves, how we act, and how we feel on a day-to-day basis. They impact our relationship with ourselves and those around us. Our inner closets are filled with a collection of other people's ideas and beliefs that we innocently took on as children and adopted as truth, unwittingly bringing them into our adult lives.

The good news is that it doesn't have to stay that way. For more than three decades, I have empowered women who once felt hopeless about their bodies and their wardrobes to become the confident, fierce, fashionable women on the outside that I know them to be on the inside. None of this requires a perfect body, but it does require the right mindset and attitude.

I invite you to bring along your curiosity, courage, and willingness, and to "try on" the following experiential exercises. Some ideas may not be the perfect fit for you in the early stages, but I assure you that combining the Silhouette Solution system with these interactive techniques has been a game changer for those who have at least tried them.

Imagine how different your world and your experiences would be if you practiced accepting and appreciating your body with gratitude, just as it is. An effective way to make peace with your body is to address your disempowering self-talk and develop a more loving relationship with your body.

Exercise #1

making peace with your body

What we think, we become.

–BUDDHA

An effective way to make peace with your body is to address your disempowering self-talk and develop a more loving relationship with yourself. (Easier said than done, I know.) As you become skilled at noticing, interrupting, and silencing your inner critic, you will not only feel more confident and comfortable in your own skin, but you will show up in the world feeling more grounded and authentic.

1. Schedule some quiet time for yourself, free from any distractions.

2. Stand in front of a full-length mirror.

3. Undress down to your underwear (or undress completely, if you're feeling brave!).

4. Make eye contact with yourself in the mirror. Calmly observe your body from head to toe. Notice the sensations present in your body as you look at yourself.

5. Notice your breathing. Is it shallow, is it deep, or are you not breathing at all? Take three deep breaths and exhale slowly. Focus on your breath. If your mind wanders (which it will), bring your focus back to your breathing.

6. Do you notice tightness anywhere? In your chest? Your back? Your neck? Keep breathing and simply notice the sensations in your body as they arise, without judgment.

7. Assess your whole body. When your eyes land on an area that you have an aversion to, pause. As you continue looking in the mirror, express out loud what society thinks your body "should" look like. ("My tummy should be flatter"; "my thighs should be thinner"; "my breasts should be bigger.")

8. Pause and notice any emotion that arises in your body as you express that "should." What emotion is present: shame, sadness, fear, hopelessness, anger, resignation? Rather than avoiding the discomfort, I encourage you to ride this emotional wave instead of denying it. Notice any other disempowering thoughts you are having and keep breathing.

9. Now, interrupt the negative thought. Replace it with a kinder, more accepting, more liberating statement about your body. ("I accept my tummy exactly as it is"; "my thighs are full, healthy, and strong"; "my breasts are perfect just as they are.")

10. Take a few moments and imagine how different your world and your experiences would be if you practiced accepting and appreciating your body with gratitude, just as it is. How would you feel? How would others see you? Take some time to try that on.

11. Repeat the exercise above and replace all your disempowering "shoulds" with what you can appreciate and accept about your body.

Notice how you feel when you express your appreciation and gratitude for your body. Really, take a few minutes and connect to that. What is present? Are you standing differently? Are you smiling? How are you breathing? Are you more relaxed? Do you feel more alive? Take a moment to notice the profound physical and emotional difference between ruminating on how you think your body *should* look and appreciating the body you do have. Allow yourself to experience the power and freedom that comes from making peace with your body.

Exercise #2

celebrate your strengths

Comparison is the thief of joy.

—THEODORE ROOSEVELT

We live in a culture of comparison. Equating yourself to others is not only detrimental to your self-confidence, it often leads to a devaluation of your innate talents and strengths. More often than not, our inner critic has us focus on all that we aren't, rather than all that we are, leading to misery and an internal sense of lack in our lives. While we can't stop society's obsession with comparisons, we can become aware of our own tendency to compare, and we can choose to celebrate our strengths instead.

Studies show that by adopting a more positive inner dialogue, you can upgrade how you think and how you feel. Practicing self-acknowledgment is a powerful tool to combat those darned critical comparisons, leaving you with more clarity and acceptance about who you truly are.

The object of this experience is to discover and allow your true, authentic self to shine through your self-doubts and comparisons. In this exercise, you will begin to acknowledge your strengths and positive attributes that often lie hidden from your view at the back of your inner closet.

1. Find a quiet place free from any distractions. Grab a pencil.

2. Take three deep breaths in and exhale slowly to center yourself.

3. Reflect on your strengths and then fill in each "I am" statement that follows with a positive attribute about yourself. Don't be shy here—go all out!

I am _____

_____

I am _____

_____

I am _____

_____

I am _____

_____

I am _____

_____

I am _____

_____

I am _____

_____

I am _____

_____

I am _____

_____

I am _____

_____

I am _____

_____

4. Whatever positive attribute comes into your mind, write it down. You can go back and edit later if you wish. What is important for this exercise is that you connect to what is great about *you*!

5. Take your time with this and then read your list out loud. Allow yourself to stay with the feelings that emerge as you read your "I am" statements. As in the last exercise, I encourage you to give some space to whatever positive or negative emotions come up. Simply sit with your experience. Observe it without judgment.

6. Notice any other contradictory thoughts and feelings that might arise and allow yourself to experience those, too, without judgment.

Keep this list with you in your purse, transfer it to your phone, or pin it on your refrigerator as a daily reminder of your amazing attributes. Feel free to add to your list as time goes on. Enjoy the clarity and freedom of connecting to and celebrating your greatness beyond self-doubts, worries, and insecurities!

I am smart
I am attractive
I am kind
I am different
I am patient
I am adventurous
I am creative
I am brave
I am intelligent
I am soulful
I am playful
I am enthusiastic
I am sincere
I am assertive
I am inventive
I am sassy
I am grateful
I am forgiving
I am accepting
I am determined
I am bold

Exercise #3

give yourself the green light

Nothing is impossible, the word
itself says "I'm possible"!
–AUDREY HEPBURN

There's something so empowering about being your own authority and making your own choices without the need for approval or permission from others—which is exactly what I want you to take away from reading this book. With self-approval comes a sense of joy and freedom to take action on what is important to you. More than an exercise, consider this a declaration of independence to confidently make your own choices. When you doubt yourself or find yourself people-pleasing or being influenced by others, refer to this green-light list and know that you are enough, exactly as you are. Find a quiet place, free from any distractions. Grab a pencil. As in the previous exercise, please write this list out using the space provided on page 35.

1. Take three deep inhalations, exhaling slowly after each to center yourself.

2. Reflect on areas of your life where you want to give yourself permission to be/do/have something specific. I've included some examples on the next page.

3. Beneath the text "I GIVE MYSELF THE GREEN LIGHT TO," list eight areas (or more, if you wish) where you are going to green-light yourself without seeking the approval or influence of others.

Accept my body
with loving kindness

Step out of my
comfort zone

Acknowledge my successes

Be open to new possibilities

Dress to express myself

Make choices that
work for me

Be comfortable in my
own skin

Feel great about myself

Wear what makes
me happy

Accept myself just as I am

Trust my own choices

Say no when I
usually say yes

Acknowledge my beauty

Say yes when I
usually say no

Be confident and happy

Experiment with
my image

Ask for what I want

As you practice giving yourself the green light, you will be able to calm the voice of your inner critic and you will develop a stronger sense of your authentic self. You'll be able to let go of negative thoughts, feel more alive, and become more confident.

You deserve to experience the joy of being *you* every day of your life, whether you're running an important business meeting or running to the grocery store. I have found these exercises to be beneficial to my clients and to myself. Looking great on the outside is only half the equation. As you transform disempowering beliefs into kinder, more accepting ones, you will shine even more brightly on the outside.

Are you ready for this journey?

Let's begin.

I give myself the green light to—

_____

_____

_____

_____

_____

_____

_____

_____

_____

_____

My mission in life is
not merely to survive,
but to thrive; and to do
so with some passion,
some compassion,
some humor, and
some style.

—MAYA ANGELOU

candid
closet .
conversations

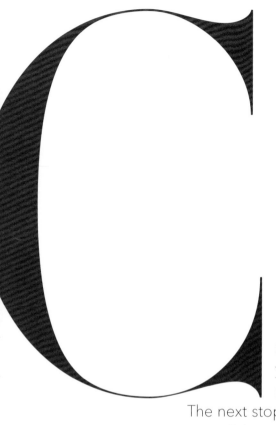

CLEARING OUT LIMITING BELIEFS FROM your inner closet creates space for new possibilities in every area of your life. The next stop on our adventure is pausing to have a candid conversation about how your actual closet is often the physical manifestation of nagging self-doubts, disempowering beliefs, and insecurities.

Being invited into a new client's wardrobe is a very personal and intimate experience that I don't take lightly. It's a bit like sneaking a peek at my client's diary and seeing her thoughts and desires. The closet is where we hide our insecurities, fears, doubts, and even wild hopes (you know—that form-fitting dress sitting in the back of your closet that's just waiting for that day you feel extra confident).

The closet is where we hide our insecurities, fears, doubts, and even wild hopes.

In my one-on-one consultations, I have peeked into every type of closet you can imagine—from those of celebrities and CEOs to those of stay-at-home moms and college students. I have seen it all! I've learned to read closets like a fortune-teller reads tea leaves, and my clients find the information I uncover to be transformational. In this chapter, I am going to guide you as you learn to read your closet, too, so you have the ability to create a wardrobe filled with beautiful clothes that you absolutely love.

To understand the link between your inner closet and your outer closet, we need to examine the relationship you have with your clothes. Just like your relationships with people, you have positive, negative, or neutral associations with every piece of clothing you own. From that cute top you wore on a successful first date to the oversize sweatshirt you wear when you've gained a few pounds, each item of clothing has a narrative. And those narratives have more of an effect on you than you know.

What's the first thing that comes to mind when I ask you about your relationship with your closet? Is your relationship with your clothes marked by joy, freedom, and ease? Or is it marred by anxiety, frustration, and confusion? Are you thrilled to walk into your closet each morning to get dressed, or are you confronted by hangers holding garments that have "problems," like being ill-fitting or unappealing? Maybe there are simply so many decisions that you *could* make that you feel overwhelmed and fail to make any at all.

Our clothes, whether they flatter us or not, can offer a strange sense of security (just like a dysfunctional or codependent relationship). We often know they don't work, yet we are reluctant to let them go. If your current clothes do not call forth confidence and joy, then those items shouldn't be taking up space in your closet (or your mind).

Imagine a closet filled with functional, beautiful clothes that flatter your body *and* your personality. Imagine wearing garments you love and treasure through many seasons. Together, we are going to confront your closet and see what it says about you. I promise that both you and your closet will be better for it.

Just like your relationships with people, you have positive, negative, or neutral associations with every piece of clothing you own. And those narratives have more of an effect on you than you know.

closet checkup

———

Let's begin with an initial assessment of your closet. During this assessment, you don't have to try anything on or remove anything just yet. (We will roll up our sleeves and edit your closet in chapter 10.) This is an observation-only exercise, where you will examine the articles of clothing you interact with daily.

I encourage you to take a radically honest look at your wardrobe by identifying clothes that fall into three distinct categories: the camouflagers (clothes we use to hide our perceived imperfections), the trends (items the fashion industry has told us we should wear to be stylish), and the approvals (clothes we wear to fit in or impress others).

When you are able to bring these unconscious influences into your conscious awareness, you will be better able to understand your relationship with your wardrobe and the limiting effect certain garments can have on you.

THE
CAMOUFLAGERS

When I refer to garments as "camouflagers," I'm not talking about military-style camo print. I'm referring to those clothes you reach for in order to conceal or hide parts of your body that you don't feel confident about. It really doesn't matter if you are size 2 or 22, 18 or 80 years old—many of us believe we have flaws that we must hide in order to look acceptable to ourselves and others. This belief is further reinforced by media, which imposes an unattainable standard of beauty. When you fail to meet the impossible standard, you are left feeling like you're not good enough. So you reach for your camouflagers—those oversize, baggy, concealing garments—to cover up your shame and embarrassment. You may not even know you are doing this, but I'm here to show you a better way.

INSIDE YOUR CLOSET

Walk into your closet and take three breaths. This will relax your entire nervous system and quiet your mind. Next, take a calm, steady look around your wardrobe. Identify the clothes—the tops, the bottoms, the dresses, the coats, the shoes—you use to hide, disguise, or conceal some part of yourself.

When you identify a few camouflagers, take a moment to think about how each garment makes you feel. Look at it. Touch it. Be radically honest. Do you love it? Do you love yourself in it? Do you feel confident wearing it? Notice your thoughts and emotions. Whatever feelings arise—positive or negative—observe and allow them. In order to heal, you must feel.

Imagine the possibility of getting dressed tomorrow—with the body you have today, not the body you wish you had. Instead of reaching for an outfit that hides parts of yourself, imagine choosing an outfit that flatters your body and makes you feel beautiful from head to toe. I guarantee you would have a better start to your day.

As you begin to bring your unconscious thoughts and feelings related to clothes into your conscious awareness, you will see how these emotions have manifested themselves in your wardrobe. You will be prepared to expand your possibilities and restructure your closet in a new, exciting way.

The fashion industry programs us to think that if we wear the latest trend, we will automatically look fashionable and attractive, but that simply is not the case.

THE
TRENDS

Fashion wouldn't be fashion without trends! Trends are at the heart of the fashion industry. While new styles, shapes, textiles, patterns, and colors are appealing, we must develop a discerning eye for which trends to include in our own wardrobes.

Born from cultural influences, such as music, art, film, sports, and celebrity culture, trends generally only last for a short time before they are replaced by new styles. The fashion industry programs us to think that if we wear the latest trend, we will automatically look fashionable and attractive, but that simply is not the case.

Throughout history, every shape and size of a woman's figure has been the "hot body" at one time or another—from waifish to curvaceous to everything in between. Here's the problem: If the current trend is a flat chest and no hips, and you have boobs, a booty, and curves, you receive a not-so-subtle message that your body isn't acceptable. Skinny jeans may be on trend, but they simply don't flatter all body types.

Keeping up with the latest fashions is a no-win situation that can cause women to ride a roller coaster of insecurity when their bodies or clothing don't align with the current moment. Today's fast fashion is actually designed to make you feel out of fashion before you've had a chance to hang your new clothes in the closet! The idea is to tap into consumers' desires, offering new "hot looks" weekly that hook us into purchasing as many garments as possible in the pursuit of feeling beautiful.

We buy more clothes than we need to keep up with the trends, only to feel inferior when those clothes don't make us look like models. But it doesn't have to be this way! You can take back control of your emotions and your wardrobe without getting knocked down by the ever-changing tsunami of trends.

INSIDE YOUR CLOSET

As you did with the camouflagers, look around your wardrobe and identify the clothes you purchased simply because they were trendy. Although these garments looked good at the moment, you now realize they have spent more time in your closet than on your body. Maybe they're already out of style! Reach out and hold one of the garments in your hands. Ask yourself: Do I love this? Do I feel confident when I wear this?

Perhaps this item looked trendy on the store mannequin. Maybe you bought it because the salesperson told you how fabulous you looked in it. Maybe all your friends were wearing this particular item, and so you wanted it, too. Whatever the reason this garment ended up in your closet, think about the story behind it. Observe the thoughts and feelings that come up and don't deny them.

I teach my clients to ask themselves one critical question regarding trends: Does this style, fabric, and color look and feel good on *my* body? I don't care if clothes are on-trend, off-trend, or in-between trends. Only when a garment fits and flatters your body *and* your personality will you look and feel fashionable.

Imagine developing your own timeless sense of style instead of navigating a revolving door of fashion trends. Take your time as you evaluate your relationship with the trends filling your closet. When you have clarity about why each garment is present, you will be better able to leave behind unattractive and unflattering styles for good.

Ask yourself:
Do I love this?
Do I feel
confident when
I wear this?

THE
APPROVALS

Approvals hang in every wardrobe. These are the clothes you purchased to fit in with or be approved by a specific group. You likely didn't even consider whether you actually liked them or felt confident wearing them. Consciously or subconsciously, you acquired this apparel to blend in with the crowd.

Approval apparel can sometimes be a benchmark by which we measure our own sense of worth and value. Filling our closets with approval apparel goes back to those youthful longings to belong and not stand out. It's why teenagers live and die by wearing name-brand clothing or the "it" item everyone's wearing. This doesn't always change when we become adults. A woman may buy an expensive designer-brand dress or pair of shoes (that goes beyond her budget) primarily because she knows it will get a thumbs-up from those in her social circles.

In my profession, I see thousands of dollars' worth of designer clothes just hanging in closets, simply because the owner wanted the prestige of wearing Louis Vuitton, Gucci, or Prada. These items weren't necessarily purchased because the owner loved how they looked; they were purchased as status symbols, to gain the approval of others. For others, approval apparel can be a type of garment—the distressed jeans everyone's wearing, the must-have sandals, or the loungewear emblazoned with a prestigious logo.

Don't misunderstand me—the instinct to want to fit in and feel accepted is natural. We all want to feel like we belong. But when you reach for garments that are more aimed toward pleasing others than pleasing yourself, you will never be fully comfortable and confident in your own skin. In fact, that discomfort may even show itself in how you think, how you behave, and how you react throughout the day.

Some professions may demand specific dress codes. I get that. And I am suggesting you can adapt that dress code to work for you. My system will show you exactly how to do it. I will teach you how to dress—at work, in social settings, or at home—in a way that casts a spotlight on the *real* you! People will want to know where you buy your clothes because you look so attractive, at ease, put together, and fashionable.

INSIDE YOUR CLOSET

Once again, take a look at your wardrobe. Select a few garments you may have unwittingly purchased to gain approval and acceptance from others. Examine the garment. Notice your thoughts and feelings. Do you love it? Do you feel like yourself when you wear it? Does this piece make you feel confident and attractive?

Self-approval is powerful. The moment you start giving yourself the green light by wearing attractive clothes that make you feel comfortable and stylish, something magical happens. You will feel more grounded and at ease with yourself. Authenticity is magnetic. You will suddenly experience others' approval because you have already done the work of approving of yourself.

Imagine choosing clothes that make *you* happy instead of garments you think will please others. Take your time as you evaluate your relationship with the approval apparel you've accumulated. When you identify why each item is in your closet, you will be better equipped to make different choices in the future. Let's look at how this change in mindset transformed one of my clients.

Imagine choosing clothes that make *you* happy instead of garments you think will please others.

CLIENT CONFESSIONS

Jeanne Confronts Her Closet

Jeanne's biggest challenge was her lack of trust in herself to coordinate outfits that were flattering, comfortable, and stylish. Her usual routine involved spending half the morning pulling apart her closet to find something she wanted to wear. When the ordeal was over, Jeanne had trashed both her closet and her confidence.

A lover of fashion, Jeanne followed trends religiously and depended upon conventional fashion advice to make her selections. Though she followed the "rules" of fashion, those rules didn't seem to translate to a wardrobe that made her feel attractive and radiant. She would look at herself in the mirror with disapproval, unable to pinpoint exactly why her clothes didn't work for her.

When I met Jeanne, I encouraged her to confront her closet and identify the clothes she'd purchased to hide her flaws or to gain approval from others. After learning my system of dressing and overhauling her closet, Jeanne discovered the kinds of clothes that flattered her body and made her feel gorgeous. We didn't have to throw out her entire closet, either! As with many of my clients, Jeanne discovered that she actually had many great pieces hiding in her wardrobe. Jeanne was thrilled when I showed her how to use what she already owned to put together fresh, modern outfits using the Silhouette Solution principles.

Today, Jeanne walks in and out of her closet feeling beautiful, attractive, and confident in her Silhouette Solution system outfits, because she is no longer a slave to trends or the approval of others.

letting go
of conventional
fashion advice

Your wardrobe should be a haven of creativity, empowerment, and self-expression. Feeling confident and empowered by your wardrobe is about balancing the proportions and geometry of your body, not about wearing the latest trends. As you develop a discerning eye, you will be able to make educated and informed decisions about your clothing and style, rather than being influenced and manipulated by the latest trends that are delivered to you by the fashion industry.

Looking fabulous, feeling confident, and stepping into your best self has little to do with hiding perceived flaws, chasing trends, or seeking approval. It has everything to do with wearing attractive, comfortable, stylish clothes that flatter *your* body and *your* personality.

The Silhouette Solution system, which you will learn about in the next chapter, offers a beautiful, empowering way to get dressed each morning. While it may be difficult to let go of some of your preconceived notions about fashion, once you learn this new way of dressing, you'll discover the freedom, joy, and ease of having dozens of flattering outfits at your fingertips.

My clients constantly tell me how transformative the Silhouette Solution system has been in their lives. They have been able to let go of self-doubts and disempowering beliefs, and they've begun to radiate a confidence that opens doors in every area of life. Never underestimate the power of a fantastic outfit to elevate your joy and emotional well-being!

I promise that you won't take this journey alone. I will be guiding you all the way, sharing the valuable tips and tricks I've learned over the course of my career as a professional stylist. Now that we've taken an initial peek into your closet, it's my pleasure to introduce you to the terrific tops and beautiful bottoms that create the foundation of the Silhouette Solution system.

Part two

The Silhouette
Solution

Simplicity is the keynote
of all true elegance.
—COCO CHANEL

terrific tops & beautiful bottoms

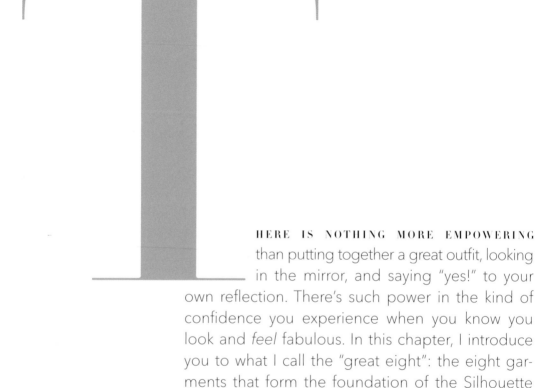

HERE IS NOTHING MORE EMPOWERING than putting together a great outfit, looking in the mirror, and saying "yes!" to your own reflection. There's such power in the kind of confidence you experience when you know you look and *feel* fabulous. In this chapter, I introduce you to what I call the "great eight": the eight garments that form the foundation of the Silhouette Solution system, the canvas upon which we will create stunning and effortless outfits.

The beauty of the Silhouette Solution is that these foundational pieces are always modern, fashionable, and affordable. The eight silhouette pieces are timeless and universally flattering, regardless of your size, age, or weight. I have designed the system for year-round use; these garments easily adapt from fall and winter to spring and summer. What may have once been a headache will transform into a speedy, simple, stress-free, and creative endeavor, while shaving minutes off your morning routine.

Once you learn my simple system, you can use it to dress for every occasion in life. You will be able to put together attractive work outfits, comfortable casual outfits, and even elegant attire for a night out on the town in no time at all. When it comes to special occasions, you will experience a new kind of ease and comfort with your wardrobe that may have prevented you from enjoying these events in the past.

So, let's meet the system!

There's such power in the kind of confidence you experience when you know you look and *feel* fabulous.

the four
terrific tops

The system starts with four essential elements to consider when building your silhouettes: the fit, fabric, color, and length. Once we get these basics dialed in and looking perfect, we can expand the system to create an infinite number of spectacular outfits using the personality pieces you will meet in part three (page 208). The result? Less stress, more joy, more confidence, more time, and *lots* of compliments.

THE
PERFECT
FIT

For the Silhouette Solution to be successful, proper fit is essential from both an aesthetic and a functional standpoint. When it comes to fit, the silhouette pieces should follow the basic shape of your body. My mantra? *Formfitting but not tight is the way to get it right.*

There are two effective ways to achieve the right fit, depending on your preference:

A SNUG FIT is when the garment clings to your body in a way that hugs your figure. This fit is perfect if you are comfortable showing off your body.

A LOOSE FIT is when the garment lays next to your skin, skimming the basic shape of your body without being tight, clingy, or constricting in any way. This shape works best for those who prefer a looser fit or don't feel 100 percent comfortable with a tighter fit.

An improper fit for the silhouettes occurs when any of the garments are so tight across your body that they create horizontal pull lines across your bust, stomach, back, or thighs, drawing unnecessary attention to those areas. Improper fit can also go to the other extreme as well, when clothes are so baggy that you look like you are wearing a sack. Regardless of your size, weight, or height, it's best to avoid excess fabric in these foundational pieces. It will make your silhouette outfit too bulky to layer over when using the personality pieces you'll learn about in chapter 6.

Formfitting
but not tight
is the way to
get it right!

THE
PERFECT FABRIC

Due to innovative advancements in textile technology, you can find the silhouettes in luxurious fabric blends that are travel-friendly and wrinkle-resistant at wonderfully affordable prices. The optimal fabrics for the silhouette pieces usually contain Lycra or spandex for stretch, which supports the "formfitting but not tight" guideline. To create flattering silhouettes, fabrics should be lightweight and smooth to the touch, untextured, drape well on your body, and feel luxurious and comfortable next to your skin.

It's the type of fabric that determines whether your silhouette pieces will be worn for work, casual outings, or dressy occasions. You may wear the same silhouette in a variety of fabrics to accommodate your different lifestyle needs. You may wear a stretch cotton tank top for working out and casual wear while using a silk, satin, or matte jersey tank top for eveningwear. Keep in mind that different fabrics can also be mixed and matched for different occasions, depending on how they are coordinated. The possibilities are endless!

For casual looks, you can generally use stretch cottons and exquisitely soft modal blends in wool, rayon, or spandex. Modal is a smooth, soft fabric similar in touch to silk or cotton. It breathes extremely well, is resistant to shrinkage, and does not fade or pill. For your professional and special-occasion wardrobe, look to more upscale fabrics like fine lightweight stretch wool, gabardine for pants and skirts, or high-quality breathable jersey knit blends with an elegant matte finish and a four-way stretch.

Your wardrobe should be a haven of creativity, empowerment, and self-expression.

THE
PERFECT
COLORS

The best colors for your silhouettes are always solid and lean toward the more neutral and darker side of the color palette. Darker colors have a slimming and elongating effect, making them a great choice for any outfit. They also provide an elegant and sleek canvas upon which you can add your favorite colors and textures later on in the process. A great starter color for the eight silhouette garments is black. Other fantastic colors to build into your silhouette wardrobe include navy, brown, dark gray, and even burgundy. For the summer months, you can lighten up your color palette with bright white, off-white, cream, or beige. And while I recommend that you start with the aforementioned colors, as you learn to navigate the system, you can create a silhouette outfit from any of your favorite colors.

ELEGANT BLACK	RICH BROWN	SOPHISTICATED NAVY	BURGUNDY
GORGEOUS GRAY	FRESH WHITE	NATURAL BEIGE	OLIVE GREEN

THE
PERFECT
LENGTH

SLEEVE LENGTHS • This system easily accommodates all seasons, temperatures, and climates. Each of the four silhouette tops can usually be found in different sleeve lengths: long-sleeved for fall and winter, and short-sleeved or sleeveless for spring and summer.

HEM LENGTHS • While women's tops come in a variety of lengths, there are two basic lengths that work superbly for the Silhouette Solution: tunic length and hip length.

Tunic length ends at the upper thigh and covers the entire torso, including the butt and crotch areas, adding what I call a "security and comfort" layer. This length creates a smooth, slimming, and elongated appearance, providing a great canvas for a kaleidoscope of looks.

Hip length, which ends a few inches below your waist at your hip bone, is perfect when you need to tuck your tops into skirts, jeans, or pants—or when you simply want a shorter top to wear over any belt loops.

The beauty of my simple yet ever-expanding system is that, while the four tops can be found in tunic and hip lengths, due to their classic and timeless nature, they come in dress length, too!

the Tank

THE TANK TOP IS A CLOSE-FITTING, LOW-CUT TOP WITH DIF-
ferent shoulder strap widths, often made of a lightweight, stretchy
fabric.

I've chosen the tank top as one of the great eight for the
Silhouette Solution because of its versatility and simplicity. Dressing
and coordinating attractive outfits becomes incredibly easy and
effortless when you use the tank as your starting point. The tank
can be worn year-round, for all occasions. From the office to the
gym, from a brunch date with friends to a dinner date with your
significant other, the tank top allows you versatility without sacri-
ficing style. For those of you living in colder climes, the tank does
double duty in the winter as a layering piece for added warmth. A
formfitting tank top provides a sleek fit. For a looser fit, try an A-line
shape that drapes beautifully next to your skin, without clinging to
the body. I personally wear a tank top almost every day. The cut,
shoulder strap width, length, and fabric will determine which type
of tank to wear and when.

THE SPAGHETTI STRAP

The spaghetti strap has very thin straps (about a quarter of an inch in width) that keep it secure over the shoulders. You know you've found a winner if it has a built-in bra. You can add a comfortable everyday smooth bra underneath, just make sure your bra color coordinates with the color of the tank. The spaghetti strap tank is usually best for small, average, and medium-framed bodies with a small- to medium-size bust and for those who want to show some skin on their upper body.

THE MEDIUM STRAP

Medium- or wide-strap tanks (with straps that are usually about one and a quarter inches wide) are for anyone who wants more coverage. The wider straps also accommodate a full-support bra without it being too visible. Again, always wear a smooth bra under your tank and match the color of your bra to the color of your tank top. The wider strap tank top is perfect for those looking for more coverage or support. The tank top is an essential building block for so many of the silhouettes, but don't worry—you will never have to expose your arms, shoulders, or chest unless you choose to.

get it right!

- Do have two lengths in your wardrobe. When in doubt, I tend to tip the scales in favor of the tunic length, which covers the complete torso and creates a smooth and elongated look.

- Do use different fabrics for different needs. You could have a stretch cotton tank top for the gym and a looser-fitting spaghetti strap tank in silk for special occasions.

- Don't wear tank tops that are too tight, as they will cut into your skin. Remember: "Formfitting but not tight is the way to get it right!"

THE Turtleneck

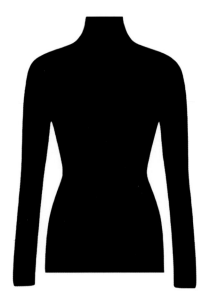

OVER THE DECADES, THE TURTLENECK HAS BEEN WORN by everyone from movie stars and artists to serious intellectuals and bohemians due to its universal, functional appeal. As soon as the cooler weather of fall sets in, the turtleneck is the perfect go-to silhouette top, and it's a great teammate for the tank top as a layering piece to create a fashionable, comfortable outfit. Think of your turtleneck as your best friend—versatile, adaptable, forgiving, and chic. A lightweight, stretch-knit turtleneck that lays softly against your body creates a slimming silhouette and becomes a canvas on which you can build a timeless look. As you mature, your turtleneck will become your best and most stylish ally, keeping you looking youthful, modern, and chic.

If you are one of those ladies who often feels cold, the turtleneck is the perfect resource. For those who overheat easily, wearing a turtleneck over a lightweight T-shirt or tank top is a great option if you need to quickly remove a layer.

As you mature, your turtleneck will become your best and most stylish ally, keeping you looking youthful, modern, and chic.

get it right!

- Do make sure your turtleneck is comfortable and not too tight around your neck.

- Make sure it pulls over your head easily.

- Do have at least two turtlenecks in your closet: one in a casual fabric and one in a more upscale fabric.

- Don't buy big, oversize turtlenecks in heavy knits—they are too bulky, and you will not be able to layer over them with the personality pieces.

- Don't panic if the turtleneck is just not right for you. All I ask is that you give it a try!

There are a few types of turtlenecks that work within the Silhouette Solution. The classic form fits the neck up to the jawline, and the mock turtleneck ends halfway up the neck with a looser fit.

Whether you are a stay-at-home mom or an in-demand executive (or both!), the turtleneck can be easily adapted for all the occasions of an active and busy life. For a dressier and more professional look, wear a turtleneck that is made of good-quality microfiber knit or a fine, lightweight wool with absolutely no extra details. The plainer, the better. For casual occasions or vacations, a stretch cotton knit or ribbed style is a more relaxed alternative. For turtleneck lovers, a short-sleeved or sleeveless turtleneck can be a superchic choice for spring and summer.

THE T-Shirt

THE FIT AND SHAPE OF YOUR T-SHIRTS MAKE ALL THE difference in the world between looking fabulous and looking just okay. My goal is for you to look great and feel beautiful whether you're going to a special event or going to bed, and that means looking fabulous, even in a T-shirt.

I don't think there's a closet that exists that isn't filled with T-shirts in all shapes, sizes, and colors. But how many do you actually wear? I bet you've collected them from all over . . . vacations, concerts, promotional giveaways.

Remember that statistic about ladies wearing only 20 percent of their clothes 80 percent of the time? It's true. And a good bit of the 80 percent you're not wearing could be all those extra T-shirts. I'm going to introduce you to T-shirts that you're going to wear 100 percent of the time and look fabulous in—but be prepared! You may be saying goodbye to many of the shirts that have been sitting on your shelves or in your drawers for months, years, or even decades.

In the Silhouette Solution system, the T-shirt is a perfect alternative if a turtleneck is too warm or feels too constricting. As long as it's the *right* T-shirt, it can be worn all year round. An elegant T-shirt is also a great layering piece that keeps you cool, just like a tank, but with more fabric and coverage for your torso and chest. Within the Silhouette Solution, T-shirts are plain in color and design, formfitting, and made of high-quality yet affordable material, like an ultra-smooth cotton/modal stretch knit or a lightweight, breathable, eco-friendly fabric like hemp, Tencel, or bamboo.

NECKLINE

The turtleneck and tank top have defined necklines, but the T-shirt has an abundance of options: round, crew, boatneck, scoop, V-neck. The list goes on. I'd like us to start with the classic crew neck, as it creates a clean and simple silhouette to build upon. You can use a V-neck or a scoop neckline for everyday wear instead of the crew neck if that's more comfortable for you, but I'd like for you to have at least one crew neck T-shirt in your closet.

get it right!

- Do wear the neckline that is most comfortable for you.

- Don't wear T-shirts covered in advertising, logos, studs, or rhinestones within the Silhouette Solution.

- Don't wear baggy or oversize T-shirts. Regardless of your size or shape, you can still wear clothes that have great fit to them, I promise. Let's celebrate the beauty and curves of our bodies!

The Ultimate Neckline

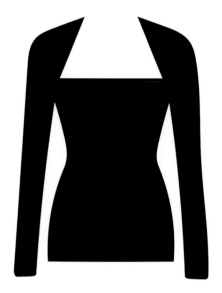

THE MAIN FEATURE OF THE FOURTH SILHOUETTE SOLUTION top is its phenomenal wide-open and somewhat squared neckline that cuts right across the bust and ends close to where the arm joins the torso, revealing both the collarbone and décolletage. There is an allure about this top that's difficult to put into words. I call it the ultimate neckline because, in my opinion, it's one of the best necklines to ever show up in women's clothing. The wide open, elegantly angular shape of this neckline magically flatters all body types. Similar to the previous three tops, you can find this beauty in all sleeve lengths and even in a dress.

My personal favorite is a brown or black dress-length ultimate neckline over straight-leg pants in the same color. The style provides ample coverage over the hips and butt for the security layer I mentioned earlier.

Unlike the other tops, the ultimate neckline will not necessarily be used for everyday wear. However, it holds an important place in your wardrobe as the item to reach for when you're getting ready for special occasions or dressy events. I've put this top on celebrities, petite ladies, and full-figured beauties of all ages, and the effect is exactly the same on all women: flattering and elegant.

By using the ultimate neckline top, you can also eliminate the headache of bringing a second outfit to work if you have to go straight from the office to a formal evening event. Simply wear this top to work with a silhouette bottom, add jewelry and a pair of high heels to dress it up for the evening, and you're good to go! You can use the ultimate neckline with your jeans to pump up the volume on your casual wardrobe, too.

get it right!

- For this top, I recommend you wear a strapless bra. The right bra should be comfortable and stay in place without causing indentation lines in your silhouette top.

- Do have at least one of these tops in your closet. On the day or evening when you need to dress up, it is a quick and easy solution for looking fabulous and will become one of your favorites.

- Don't wear an ultimate neckline that's too low. We don't want any wardrobe malfunctions here!

ow that we have covered the four tops, it goes without saying that no outfit is complete without the perfect bottom. Whatever the current trend, I doubt leaving the house bottomless will ever catch on!

To create attractive, practical, and functional silhouettes, you need only pair these four tops with their spouses, the four universally flattering silhouette bottoms. The addition of these carefully curated bottoms will create a flattering, slimming, and elongating appearance that will make you look spectacular and feel beautiful. Once we put those together, we'll further develop the system with shoes and personality pieces to create your unique style personality.

the four
beautiful bottoms

The fab four universally flattering bottoms of the Silhouette Solution consist of two pants styles and two skirt styles that will meet every possible dressing need you may have. Just like the tops, there are some essential guidelines to address and follow regarding the fit, fabric, and length of our bottoms. This ensures that you will always look stylish and elegant while feeling fully comfortable and empowered in your clothes.

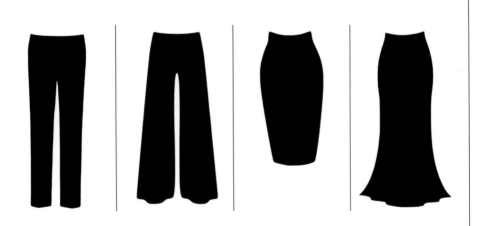

THE
PERFECT FIT

No matter the occasion or function, fit is as important as fashion. You want your pants and skirts to fit your life and your hips correctly. Poorly fitting bottoms are not only uncomfortable, they're visually unappealing and will attract negative attention. To ensure the correct fit, check to see if they are:

TOO TIGHT IN THE WAIST • Your pants and skirts should drape easily and naturally over your waist without cutting into your skin. According to one neurologist in Chicago, some people suffer from what he calls "tight pants syndrome," which can cause abdominal pain, numbness, and even heartburn. His study found that women are choosing to wear pants that are up to three inches too small in the waist, which can cause lasting physiological effects. It's more important to have the right fit for your body than to be able to squeeze into a specific size just for the sake of having a certain number in your closet.

TOO TIGHT IN THE HIPS • When your pants or skirts are too tight in the hips, the first issue will be a visible panty line. In my opinion, there is no worse fashion blunder than seeing the complete landscape of your underwear through your clothing. Pants that are too tight in the hips will also cause the front zipper to warp and pull; wearing a skirt that is too tight in the hips will cause it to ride up your body. The solution is to simply size up. Don't let the number on a tag determine your self-worth or your mood.

TOO TIGHT IN THE THIGHS • If your pants are too tight in the thighs, they will grip your legs in such a way that the fabric will not be able to drape or lay flat against your skin. To make sure there is some breathing room, perform the "pinch-an-inch" test. If you can't pinch an inch of extra fabric on your thighs, your pants may be on the verge of being too tight and are at risk of pulling apart at the seams. Jeans are designed and constructed to fit your thighs snugly, so ignore the pinch-an-inch rule when it comes to your jeans.

TOO TIGHT IN THE CROTCH • If you can see the shape of your—ahem—*lady parts* through the pants, they're most definitely too tight in the crotch. The pants are either way too tight or the style does not fit your body shape. Again, neither is good for your health. Size up, try a different pair of pants, or, if these are pants you already have, wear your tunic-length top to cover the butt and crotch areas.

THE
PERFECT FABRIC

The basic fabric types mentioned for tops also apply to bottoms. Key words to remember are *lightweight, smooth, stretch,* and *untextured.* One of my favorite all-purpose fabrics is a breathable synthetic knit stretch jersey that has an elegant matte finish and a beautiful drape. It is also easily washable, travel-friendly, and wrinkle-resistant, making it super versatile. With its high-quality look, this fabric will work for all your lifestyle needs when coordinated correctly.

THE
PERFECT COLOR

The colors for the bottoms must always match the colors of the tops to create a clean, figure-elongating, monochromatic line upon which you can add your favorite personality pieces. If you wear a black top, always coordinate it with a black bottom. If you wear a white top, always coordinate it with a white bottom. You get the picture.

Now, let's meet the partners to our exquisite and practical tops!

THE Straight-Leg Pant

SEASON AFTER SEASON, I'VE CONVERTED MANY SELF-PROFESSED SKIRT lovers into pants aficionados, demonstrating the wonderful and stylish possibilities the right pants have to offer. Besides being fabulously functional, a straight-leg pant, when worn correctly, is one of the best power pieces your wardrobe has to offer. It is super practical while still being sexy and feminine. Many of us have had some frustrating shopping expeditions in search of the perfect pants for our body shape. Now, your search is over! No matter whether you are short or tall, heavy or thin, or simply confused by all the pants styles available, the cut and shape of straight-leg pants or jeans make them universally flattering and resistant to ever-fluctuating trends.

The straight-leg pant or jean has a flat front with no pleats. The diameter of the leg opening is generally the same width from the knee to the hem. A critical design element of this piece is the length of the pant. It must extend past the ankle to create an elongating appearance for the leg. It does not taper into a skinny pant, and it is not cropped, but I don't mind if it has a slight flare. While skinny pants can be a great silhouette piece and are wildly popular, if they are worn too tight (which is often the case), they tend to make a person look heavier than they are.

The Silhouette Solution's straight-leg pant has minimum detail. It doesn't have decorative zippers, embroidery, studs, or fancy stitching; the pants can be a simple stretch pull-on style or have a front or side zipper. My preference is to have no side pockets, as they tend to pull open, but I'll leave that up to you. The key is to keep the look and line of your silhouette garments simple, sleek, and smooth.

If you can't live without your leggings, they can be incorporated into the system. However, I encourage you to try a pair of straight leg stretch pants, which flatter many women because they create more balance between the upper and lower body.

get it right!

- Find a pair of simple straight-leg pull-on pants (without zippers) with a stretch waistband that is both comfortable and breathable for casual or weekend wear. The right kind can also be used for exercise.

- You'll also want a pair of lightweight to medium-weight stretch straight-leg classic blue jeans.

- For work or dressing up, get a more tailored straight-leg pant in an upscale fabric.

THE Wide-Leg Pant

NOW THAT YOU'VE MET MY DARLING, DEPENDABLE STRAIGHT-LEG PANT, it's time to meet her free-spirited and easygoing cousin, the wide-leg pant. Originally worn by fearless, iconic women like designer Coco Chanel in the Roaring Twenties, they became a bold alternative for women wanting to look chic, modern, and confident without wearing traditional, old-fashioned skirts.

Sophisticated, comfortable, and elegant, a wide-leg pant fits the hips and waist with a nice, roomy, wide leg that increases in width to the hemline. A tailored design with a more substantial fabric is called a wide leg, while a flowy, lightweight fabric with an even wider hem is known as a palazzo pant.

The most practical style for everyday wear is a lightweight pull-on pant with a stretch waistband. The dressier version of the wide-leg pant may have a front or side zipper. This beautiful and versatile basic is probably the most controversial of the great eight silhouette pieces, because many women assume they're going to look short or dumpy due to the wide leg. They have been led to believe that only tall, slender women can wear wide legs. Nothing could be further from the truth. A wide leg does not automatically equate to you looking wide or short. Because of the graceful and elegant way in which this pant drapes on the body, it magically minimizes and slims. If you ever have one of those days when you are feeling bloated, wear your wide-leg pants. You can be stylish and chic while feeling as free as a bird!

For casual wear, there isn't a more versatile bottom. You can wear it during the day and transition it into casual eveningwear. Great for moms on the go and busy professionals alike, wide-leg pants are an uplifting style alternative to jeans or sweatpants. They are a perfect item to pack for summer vacation and can easily transition from poolside to fancy dinner. For formal events, your solution is simple. Wear the evening version of your wide-leg pants in an elegant silk, satin, or matte jersey, and pair them with the ultimate neckline or an evening tank and a personality piece for a spectacular, comfortable, and stylish look.

get it right!

- Try this pant with a flat or sandal. Nothing is more glamorous than a colorful pedicure and a bejeweled sandal to offset this look.

- Wide-leg pants come in several widths at the hem. Choose the one that works for you.

- Hem to a length that covers the ankles—a quarter to a half an inch above the floor is perfect. Take into account the height of the shoe you plan to wear.

- Don't wear chunky shoes or boots with lightweight palazzo pants (but it's okay to do so with a structured wide-leg pant).

THE Pencil Skirt

FIRST DESIGNED OUT OF NECESSITY IN THE 1940S TO SAVE PRECIOUS fabric rations during World War II, Christian Dior went on to showcase the pencil skirt as a fashion item in his 1954 collection. It has remained a style staple ever since. The pencil skirt can be your go-to Silhouette Solution power piece for work, casual, and dressy occasions alike. It will make you feel elegant, assertive, and feminine—that is, if it's done right!

There are two versions of the pencil skirt that work within the Silhouette Solution. The first is the traditional slim-fitting pencil skirt. This skirt has a straight, narrow cut, tailored for a close fit, with a hem that ends at the knee. The other option, also slim, falls at the knee with a flounce hem, to add a little more flair while still looking sophisticated. Both styles work superbly depending upon your personal preference.

Length is a huge factor in pulling off a great pencil skirt silhouette, especially in a professional setting. Your skirt hem should never be more than one inch above your knee. And while I recommend the pencil skirt primarily for professional wear, you can also wear a stretch pull-on pencil skirt, a denim pencil skirt, or even a leather pencil skirt for your casual, weekend, and vacation wardrobes. In this context, you can wear it much shorter and sportier while still looking superchic and modern.

When you need dressy or special-occasion attire and you don't want to search for a cocktail dress or gown, a dressier knee-length pencil skirt in a matte jersey, silk, or satin is perfect to pair with a sophisticated turtleneck or the ultimate neckline top. I once bought a gorgeous black sequined pencil skirt and wore it with an elegant black turtleneck, a sexy high-heeled sandal, and some statement jewelry to a party. It was an *extremely* last-minute invitation, but because I understand how to use the Silhouette Solution and have stocked my wardrobe with the right pieces, it was easy to march into my closet and quickly whip up a stunning look. We are all stretched for time these days, and the Silhouette Solution is the answer when it's necessary to put together an elegant outfit at the last minute.

get it right!

- Do try to find a pencil skirt with a flouncy bottom for some added flair.

- Do consider adding a more casual pull-on-style to look stylish and feel comfortable—even while you run errands.

- Don't wear your pencil skirt too tight or too short in a professional setting. The hem should never fall higher than one inch above your knee.

- Don't be afraid to go up a size if necessary to get the right fit.

THE Maxi Skirt

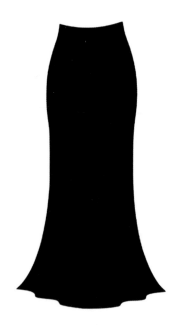

THE MAXI SKIRT IS AN ANKLE-LENGTH OR FLOOR-LENGTH skirt that strikes an equally beautiful balance between casual and practical glamour. My favorite style is the mermaid or trumpet shape, which is comfortably formfitting from the hips to the knee and flares out slightly to the floor, allowing for ease of movement. It is very flattering regardless of body shape and is a beautiful building block upon which we can add superb personality pieces. This style of skirt can be worn by women of all ages and adds an instant element of coolness.

A word of warning: These days, fabrics are not what they used to be. Even expensive clothes are often made with inexpensive fabrics, which may not be apparent at first glance. A woman can be dressed stylishly in a maxi skirt, but if it's made from cheap fabric, you can sometimes see right through the skirt when the light

hits it in a particular way. I have witnessed this too many times, and the wearer is completely oblivious that she is walking around in a see-through skirt! A good way to test for this in the dressing room is simply to stand in front of the mirror, feet planted firmly apart, and look closely to determine if you can see the shape of your legs and light coming through the fabric.

Maxi skirts are a great casual option. Go for a stretch cotton, rayon jersey, or microfiber blend with a stretch waistband—comfort is key here. Wear this skirt with any of your four tops for an endless array of styles. In the workplace I suggest wearing a ballerina length, which ends at the ankle, in a slightly heavier weighted fabric.

get it right!

- If you're thinking you can't pull off a maxi skirt, I assure you that it's universally flattering!

- Hem it to a length that is comfortable. Ballerina length hits just at the ankle and is great for work. Floor length hits about an inch above the floor and adds a dressier vibe, even in casual settings.

- Watch out for visible panty lines.

a-line or pleated

If you find that the pencil or maxi skirt just isn't for you, try an A-line or pleated version. While the pencil skirt and the maxi skirt (pages 78 and 80) do the most to visually lengthen your body, I want you to be 100 percent comfortable in your silhouettes. Wear a heel if you wish to add height. The Silhouette Solution can be versatile and work with clothes you already have in your closet.

A-LINE   PLEATED

The four tops and four bottoms that I've out-lined form the foundation of the Silhouette Solution system. These pieces will become more than just clothes in your closet: They are confidence-builders, stress-relievers, and time-savers. These are the pieces you will reach for every time you get dressed as the starting point to build a fabulously function wardrobe.

never say never

At this point, you may have some opinions about the garments I have outlined in this chapter. In fact, I expect it. You may be thinking, "I don't wear all black," or "I could never wear a pencil skirt!" You may even be thinking that this system isn't for you.

This type of reaction is not uncommon when I first introduce women to my transformational system. Remember, these eight garments are the building blocks and foundational pieces of a much bigger picture that I am confident will thrill you by the end of this book. I ask you to set aside your doubts, darling, until I have introduced you to the whole system. As you give it a chance, you may find that your negative opinions about certain garments radically change, as has happened for so many of my clients.

I encourage you to open your mind to the possibilities and be willing to try new things. Keep in mind that these eight universally flattering pieces may not all turn out to be your favorites. For example, my daily go-to pieces are a tank top and a pair of straight-leg or wide-leg pants. Putting on those pieces is as automatic as brushing my teeth. I simply couldn't imagine my life without them!

As you get to know the Silhouette Solution, you will decide which of the eight will be *your* everyday pieces—and the results may surprise you! One client had never worn a pair of wide-leg pants before, but she came to adore the garment after seeing how amazing she looked in a completely coordinated Silhouette Solution outfit. Trust me when I say that you will be able to use this simple system to transform your wardrobe and your confidence.

In the next chapter, we are going to meet the eight universally flattering shoe styles that complement and complete the foundational pieces of the Silhouette Solution. You will learn how just a few shoe styles can transform the entire look of an outfit, and how the right shoe can elevate your mood and your day. Once you learn how easy it is to create a stunning silhouette using a terrific top, a beautiful bottom, and the perfect pair of shoes, you'll be amazed at the world of stylish and flattering options that will open up for you as we add in the personality pieces. And you'll be even more amazed at the peace of mind, confidence, and joy that comes with getting dressed each day. Read on and discover how these shoe styles, in partnership with the tops and bottoms outlined above, can create 96 fabulously functional outfits.

ALTERNATE ALERT!

additional options

The Silhouette Solution includes eight garments as a starting point. As you learn the system, you may find yourself inspired to create your own silhouettes. I encourage you to experiment and play around with what works for you. For example, an alternative summer outfit could be a pair of white shorts and a white tank top, or black shorts and a black tank. While these eight garments create endless outfit options, you are not limited to these eight. They are simply a starting point. Whatever you choose, make sure it is the same color on top and bottom and that it flatters your body type.

Shoes transform your body
language and attitude. They lift
you physically and emotionally.
–CHRISTIAN LOUBOUTIN

stepping out in style

HOES PLAY AN EXCITING AND TRANSFOR-
mational role in the Silhouette Solution
system. Their purpose—besides making you
look gorgeous—is twofold. First, as you pair them
with the terrific tops and beautiful bottoms, they
complete the foundational canvas of the Silhouette
Solution. Second, a great pair of shoes can enhance
your mood, elevate your confidence, and even
transform your day. On those days when you feel
stuck in your inner closet and you can't quiet that
negative voice, a gorgeous pair of shoes will lift
your spirits and your style. Make no mistake: Shoes
are powerful.

A different shoe can change the entire look of
your outfit. It can transform your style from casual to
dressy, from playful to glamorous. When it comes

to the Silhouette Solution, I have learned that less is often more. A closet packed with dozens of shoes doesn't necessarily equal increased versatility and style. In fact, the opposite is often true, as having more shoes usually creates physical and emotional clutter that causes confusion, stress, and anxiety.

For the Silhouette Solution, I've narrowed down footwear to eight styles: four flats and four heels. I return to these eight styles each season for one simple reason: They work! These eight curated styles will simplify your dressing routine and help you step out with confidence, regardless of the occasion.

A gorgeous pair of shoes will lift your spirits and your style. Make no mistake: Shoes are powerful.

the four
fabulous flats

If you want to elevate your confidence while keeping your feet firmly on the ground, wear a beautiful pair of flats. When it comes to comfort and timeless elegance, flats are queen! Whether a boot, a dress shoe, or a sandal, flats offer style, comfort, and function. The four flats in my system harmonize beautifully with and add balance to the four tops and four bottoms, creating sublime silhouettes.

THE Flat Sandal

STEPPING INTO AN EXQUISITE AND ELEGANT PAIR OF SANDALS IS LIKE wearing jewelry on your feet. They are a perfect choice for warm summer days and allow your feet to breathe. To be clear, I'm not talking about Birkenstocks or hiking sandals. I have nothing against those styles (or maybe I do!), but I suggest you reserve those for hiking or household chores.

Sandals come in a variety of designs, from simple flip-flops to strappy, bejeweled varieties. I suggest treating your feet to a pedicure so you can step out in confidence when wearing sandals. For a woman who isn't comfortable displaying her toes, closed-toe sandals are another stunning option. You'll look summery without feeling exposed.

For summer, black and metallic varieties always look superb. When I find a winning sandal, I buy it in bulk—one black, one gold, one silver—and wear it season after season. However, if you're on a budget, stick with black for dark silhouettes and a versatile metallic (gold or silver) pair.

THE Ballet Flat

GRACEFUL, PRACTICAL, AND FEMININE, THE BALLET FLAT IS ONE OF the most useful shoes you can have in your closet because of its versatility, comfort, and classic style.

Like every shoe you will meet in this chapter, a ballet flat can be worn for work, around town, and for dressy occasions. This darling shoe adds just the right amount of polish to any look without being pretentious.

Ballet flats come in a variety of styles, so you can experiment to find the one that looks best on you. Inspired by authentic ballerina slippers, classic round-toe ballet flats cover the toes completely with a small lace-up bow on the top. Low-cut ballet flats reveal toe cleavage for a sexier style. There are also pointed-toe, square-toe, and cap-toe varieties, as well as the lovely d'Orsay (or two-piece) ballet flats that have only the toe and heel cup. You can even find an athletic version of a ballet flat with a rubber sole that molds to the foot.

For special occasions or eveningwear, ballet flats can be satin, velvet, or even sequined, adding understated elegance to your dressy ensembles. If you don't already have this little gem in your wardrobe, I'd suggest starting with a basic black ballet flat made of soft suede, leather, or fabric. After that, if you fall in love with this beauty, as I have, you may wish to expand into other colors or metallic hues.

the smart loafer

If you don't prefer ballet flats, opt for the comfortable, classic loafer. Look for a black suede or an embossed mock crocodile in black or brown to look classy and elegant. My personal favorite is black suede with chunky soles. They look like dress shoes but feel like sneakers.

the stylish sneaker

These days, most women find themselves constantly on the move. They need their clothes, and their shoes, to function in multiple settings. While sneakers are great for athletic endeavors, they can often "cross-train" in other areas of our lives as well. While I haven't included a sneaker as one of the great eight shoes, feel free to include a pair in your closet to add a sporty, relaxed vibe to your silhouette outfits. Choose a sneaker that matches your silhouette for a look that's streamlined from head to toe. For a black silhouette outfit, choose a simple, unembellished black sneaker. Wear a white sneaker with a white silhouette.

THE Flat Ankle Boot

QUEEN VICTORIA MADE FLAT ANKLE BOOTS ALL THE RAGE IN 1851. Practical and comfortable, with an understated elegance, it's easy to see why they became an enduring trend. This boot is close-fitting with a clean and sleek look (which gives it a lifetime membership to the Silhouette Solution). Elastic side panels create a close and comfortable fit. Sometimes this boot has a loop or tab of fabric on the back of the boot, which allows it to be pulled on easily.

This boot, also known as the Chelsea boot for being a favorite of the "Chelsea set" in 1950s England, is attractive, comfortable, and stylish—perfect for cool weather and travel when you plan to be on your feet a lot. Flat ankle boots in black suede work superbly with straight-leg pants for work, and with jeans or a maxi skirt for casual wear. This boot also looks great in classic leather, microfiber, elegant faux crocodile, or even rubber, in the case of a stylish rain boot.

THE Riding Boot

MEET THE FIRST COUSIN OF THE FLAT ANKLE BOOT. SIMILAR IN THE foot and heel shape, this boot extends up the leg to just below the knee. Associated with elite equestrian sports, such as polo, show jumping, and horse racing, riding boots send a message of style and luxury. The design features of traditional riding boots are primarily based on functionality, but they have become a timeless fashion staple for women's wardrobes.

In colder seasons, this boot's rugged elegance looks unexpectedly brilliant with a knee-length pencil skirt, a black turtleneck, and gold or silver jewelry. For a posh, equestrian vibe, tuck a narrow straight-leg pant inside the boot. Start with a classic leather riding boot that hits just below the knee to elongate the leg and make you appear taller. The top of the boot should fit smoothly (but not too tightly) against your leg. If you can slip more than three fingers between the top of the shoe and your leg, the boot is too wide.

the four
fabulous heels

There is something magical about a pair of heels. They can instantly make you feel more sophisticated, confident, and alluring. A good pair of heels will elevate any look and is, without a doubt, one of the greatest assets in your wardrobe!

Not all heels are alike, and finding the right height and style to match your personality and lifestyle is important. Before I go into too much detail, let me first introduce you to five heel types so that you can strut your style wearing the most comfortable and appropriate heel for you.

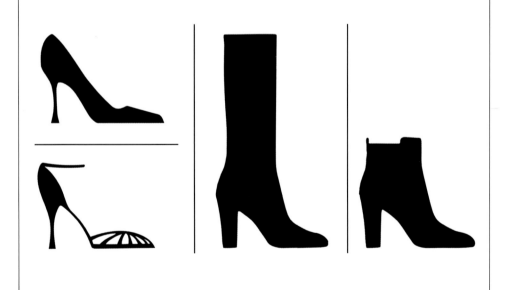

THE BLOCK HEEL • This practical, everyday heel gives height without putting strain on the foot or the body as you walk. This classic heel is easy to identify because it has the same width from top to bottom. The block heel can be a high heel, as on a heeled pump, or a shorter version, as you might see on a flat ankle boot.

THE CUBAN HEEL • This modern, attractive low heel is similar to the block heel but has a slightly tapered back and a straight front. At approximately an inch and a half in height, the Cuban heel is a great compromise between a high heel and a flat, and offers an edgy, modern silhouette.

THE PLATFORM HEEL • This shoe has an extremely thick sole designed to raise the foot off the ground. The right platform heel can add several inches of height without putting extra stress on the ball of your foot.

THE STILETTO HEEL • This sexy and sophisticated shoe has a tall, very thin heel. A stiletto heel can range anywhere from two inches—known as the kitten heel—to a bold, sexy five inches!

THE WEDGE HEEL • While not truly a heeled shoe, this elevated shoe provides an alternative for women who are unable to, or choose not to, wear other types of heels. The elevated heel and toe of the shoe are joined in one piece, providing the foot with ample support.

THE Pump

A SOPHISTICATED BLACK SUEDE PUMP IS THE EPITOME OF ELE-
gance. This classic, feminine shoe can transform the way you look and feel
in an instant. A pump covers both sides of the foot, as well as the toe
and heel. A high-heeled pump makes the pencil skirt look exquisite, adds
feminine allure to straight-leg pants, and dresses up a maxi skirt. While
I wear flats for most of my daily routine, when I slip on a pair of heels,
something magical happens: I feel elegant, feminine, and empowered. I
unconsciously pull my tummy in, roll my shoulders back, and extend my
neck. Wearing an elegant pump to work sends a message of professional
authority, but it's also a wonderful choice to dress up jeans for a night out.

THE Strappy Sandal

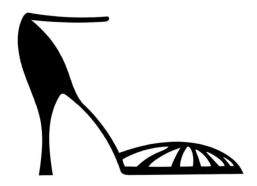

I LIKE TO THINK OF THE STRAPPY SANDAL AS THE BIKINI OF shoes: it's equally flirty and revealing. Similar to the flat sandal, this open style of footwear is held to the sole of the foot by straps. But this sandal elevates, baby! Greater elevation equals greater elongation, which means you look taller and thinner.

The strappy sandal can be found in a variety of heel heights, and if you don't want your toes exposed, go with a closed-toe style. For the working professional, a high-heeled sandal can easily transition your outfit from day to evening and add an instant pop of glamour. You can also wear them with pants for added elegance.

Start by adding a black strappy sandal to your wardrobe, then think about adding a gold or silver metallic pair for a touch of pizazz! This sandal will be a must-have for special occasions and can add the finishing touch to summer and eveningwear.

THE Heeled Ankle Boot

HEELED ANKLE BOOTS, ALSO KNOWN AS BOOTIES, ARE HIP AND SWANKY. If you want to add a stylish kick to your outfit and appear tall, slim, and modern, this beauty will help you achieve that look. Once considered an occasionally worn piece, usually partnered with pants, the heeled ankle boot has become a wardrobe staple that you can successfully wear with dresses and skirts.

High-heeled booties cover the entire foot and end at the ankle or just above it. They can be open-toed or closed-toed and can be worn year-round, but they work especially well in autumn and winter. Booties come in a variety of heel styles and heights—from stilettos, for a dressier look, to the lower Cuban or block heel, for a more casual vibe.

I have two favorites. The first is a black matte suede, two-inch stiletto with a pointed toe and a back or side zipper. This boot's sleek shape gives a polished feel to any outfit without killing your feet. My other favorite is a black suede or leather Cuban heeled bootie, which is perfect for work or a casual night on the town. The style of bootie you choose—chunky, funky, open-toed, closed-toed, block heel, or stiletto—depends entirely on your personal style.

THE Heeled Knee Boot

HEELED KNEE-HIGH BOOTS ARE POWERFUL, FUNCTIONAL, AND SEXY. There's just something about a woman in a high-heeled black knee boot that communicates she knows who she is and where she's going. First cousin to the high-heeled ankle boot, this beauty does wonders to create a look that is both upscale and powerful. Extending from the ankle to just below the knee, this boot is functional and stylish for autumn, winter, and even spring.

My favorite heeled knee boot is black suede, with a stiletto heel for a dressier look or a Cuban heel for a more relaxed vibe. This boot is also fabulous in a micro-fiber fabric, leather, faux leather, or faux stretch suede. If you get a classic cut (no embellishments, not too pointed, not too rounded), you can wear it season after season.

choosing the perfect fit

As I mentioned in the previous chapter, *fit is as important as fashion*. This is never truer than when it comes to selecting shoes. Each of the eight shoes you just met can be found in a variety of styles and fits. It's essential to find a version that is comfortable while reflecting your unique style (which I will help you discover in chapter 6), as an uncomfortable shoe can ruin your whole day.

As you shop, keep in mind that your foot should fit comfortably in the shoe, with ample space for your toes. Notice if the ball and arch of your foot feel supported. When you walk, you should feel no pain or pinching. Always check your comfort level by taking a new shoe for a test run in the store (or at home, if you buy online). If a shoe is not comfortable the first time you wear it, chances are that it won't feel better over time.

Don't buy shoes that are too big or too small. I once purchased a pair of irresistible silver sandals, knowing they were half a size too small. But they were the last pair in the store, and I couldn't imagine life without them! As beautiful as they are, they have not seen the outside of my closet more than a couple of times.

FABRICS & COLORS

A shoe's fabric will determine whether it works with a silhouette for work, casual wear, or a special occasion. You can wear the same style of shoe in different fabrics to accommodate different outfits. For example, you can wear suede, leather, or microfiber for work, and save satin, sequins, or velvet for formal events.

Black suede is the fabric I most often recommend. The subtle matte finish of suede is similar in color and texture to the fabric of the silhouette garments, which creates continuity and a streamlined look. High-quality microfiber fabrics also work superbly. They have the added benefit of being waterproof and easy to clean. For knee-high boots, stretch fabrics slide over your calf effortlessly while looking sleek and elegant.

When it comes to color, your shoes should always match the color of your Silhouette Solution outfits. If you choose a black top and bottom for your silhouette outfit, wear black shoes to elongate your look. If you wear a brown silhouette, wear brown shoes. Choose the style and color of each of the eight shoes that works for your personal style. Keep in mind that metallics, like gold and silver, serve as a neutral alternative for the flat and heeled sandals.

stepping out

These eight versatile shoes blend with the Silhouette Solution garments to create a streamlined and stylish look from head to toe. They allow you to quickly and effortlessly change your look. Instead of facing the overwhelming clutter of shoes you rarely wear, you will experience joy when your closet is stocked with the perfect shoes for your lifestyle and events.

In the next chapter, I'll show you how to combine the four tops, four bottoms, and eight shoes into an amazing number of gorgeous and fabulously functional silhouette outfits. I have relied on these flattering, affordable pieces for decades. I love to look great, and I don't love spending a lot of time or money to get there! I can't wait to provide you with the knowledge and tools to upgrade your look and give you the confidence to step out in style.

Fashion is very important.
It is life-enhancing and, like
everything that gives pleasure,
it is worth doing well.
–VIVIENNE WESTWOOD

combining your silhouettes

CHRISTY WAS OVERJOYED TO ARRIVE in Los Angeles from Australia to visit her uncle and explore the city. There was one problem: The airline had lost her luggage, leaving her with only the clothes on her back. She was assured that her luggage would arrive within twenty-four hours, but three days later, it had still not been recovered. Her uncle John, a good friend of mine, called me, asking if I could help.

I quickly agreed. Christy didn't have the budget to purchase a completely new wardrobe, nor did she need one for her trip. She simply needed a few outfits to tide her over until her luggage was found.

I picked her up, and we headed to one of my favorite discount stores. Having just met her, I knew nothing about thirty-something Christy—her style, her insecurities, or her preferences. Inside the store, we had a quick consultation, and she pointed out the go-to pieces of her casual lifestyle wardrobe—skinny jeans, a loose printed blouse, and sandals or sneakers. When I offered to help her experiment with some attractive new outfits that were variations on her usual choices, she agreed.

We started scanning the racks, and I quickly selected several tops and bottoms of the great eight foundational pieces. On the way to the dressing room, I grabbed a pair of low-heeled ankle boots and metallic flat sandals.

First, Christy tried on a straight-leg dark denim jean instead of her usual skinny style. She was surprised and delighted to find that they not only felt amazingly comfortable but also that they made her petite frame look taller and slimmer. Next, I added a black elongated tank top that covered her hips and butt, creating a slimming effect. Finally, she slipped on a pair of comfortable black suede ankle boots to complete a striking and flattering silhouette. We added a light open-front drape cardigan to create a modern outfit that could be worn for a casual hangout and added

some gold accessories and exquisite gold sandals for a casual dress event. As I coordinated a few more silhouette outfits, Christy's excitement and enthusiasm grew. Not only did she love how she looked, but her upgraded style instantly enhanced her confidence as well. She couldn't wait to start enjoying her vacation. And, decked out in her new Silhouette Solution outfits, she really didn't care if her lost suitcase ever showed up (which it did—a week later)!

Christy is one of many success stories I've experienced as I've helped women transform their dressing routines and lives using the Silhouette Solution. You've met the great eight— the eight garments that form the foundation of the system. You've also met the four flats and four heels that comprise the flattering footwear to complete stunning, effortless silhouettes. Now that you know these 16 pieces, it's time to learn how to combine them into complete outfits.

Each of the four tops coordinates with the four bottoms, giving you 16 different outfit possibilities. (For example, you can pair the elongated tank with palazzo pants or a maxi skirt for two different looks.) Then, combine these 16 spectacular silhouettes with the shoes to create more than 96 complete outfits. These foundational outfits form the base that we will build upon.

These 96 silhouette outfits are modern, comfortable, versatile, age-defying, and affordable. They work regardless of your height, your weight, or the shape of your body. Even when your inner closet is screaming, "I can't wear that!" these outfits work. I have used them for decades, and I will continue using them, because they turn getting dressed into an effortless, confidence-building experience that becomes the easiest part of your day.

Once you understand the important role that each of the foundational tops, bottoms, and shoes plays in the Silhouette Solution, you will see how they act as the blank canvas upon which you can develop your personal style.

The way I've designed this system, it's nearly impossible to make a mistake coordinating a silhouette outfit. Each piece works with all the other pieces, so whether you're preparing for a day at the office or an elegant event, getting dressed is simple and stress-free. Choose a top, choose a bottom, and select a shoe, and you'll have coordinated a perfect foundational outfit. In the next chapter, I'll introduce you to the awesome world of personality pieces, which will allow you to expand outfit possibilities and express your unique and individual style.

These 96 silhouette outfits are modern, comfortable, versatile, age-defying, and affordable. They work regardless of your height, your weight, or the shape of your body.

put together a silhouette in a second

1. **CONSIDER WHAT YOU ARE DRESSING FOR:**
   work, a casual hangout, or a special occasion.

2. **CHOOSE WHAT TO WEAR AS YOUR TOP:**
   tank, turtleneck, T-shirt, or ultimate neckline.

3. **DECIDE WHAT TO WEAR AS YOUR BOTTOM:**
   straight-leg pants, wide-leg pants, pencil skirt, or
   maxi skirt.

4. **PICK A PAIR OF SHOES:**
   ballet flat, ankle boot, riding boot, or sandal (in a
   heel or a flat).

How to Incorporate the Shoes

The eight shoe styles allow you to easily and quickly change up your silhouette outfit. You can transform from casual to dressy, from office to evening, from cold weather to warm weather by simply changing your shoes. Before choosing a shoe style to coordinate with your silhouette outfit, think about how you want to look and feel and what you want to communicate through your appearance. Do you want to project a casual and relaxed feeling, or do you want to convey a more upscale vibe? A ballet flat dresses down an outfit, while a heel dresses it up.

work silhouette outfits

If you have ever had a before-work crisis in the closet (and who hasn't?), using the silhouettes will streamline your routine and change your life. Regardless of whether your work environment is corporate, casual, or work from home, the Silhouette Solution can help you get dressed for your workday with ease.

For work, your go-to silhouette tops will be the tank, the T-shirt, and the turtleneck. Choose any of the four bottoms. For a corporate environment, you might wear a pencil skirt or a straight-leg pant, with a dressy T-shirt and a heeled pump. If your work environment is really casual, wear the straight-leg jean with a tank and a flat ankle boot or sandal. Remember that the fabric often determines how dressy a garment is. For a formal office environment, wear dressier fabrics such as fine wool gabardine blends, smooth microfibers, and matte jersey knits. Stretch cotton blends, dark denim, modal blends, wool, and rayon work well for a more casual workplace.

Choose your shoe based on your individual needs and personal style. If you do a lot of walking during your day, a ballet flat, a smart loafer, or a flat ankle boot is a chic yet comfortable choice. A high-heeled pump or heeled ankle boot can add polish for a meeting or presentation.

More Examples for the Workplace

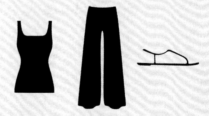

CASUAL WORKPLACE
- T-Shirt
- Straight-Leg Jean
- Heeled Ankle Boot

WORK FROM HOME
- Tank
- Wide-Leg Pant
- Flat Sandal

More Examples
for Casual Occasions

- Ultimate Neckline
- Straight-Leg Jeans
- Heeled Ankle Boot

- Casual Tank
- Casual Maxi Skirt
- Ballet Flat

casual silhouette outfits

———

Like an artist's canvas, the silhouettes form the base outfit you can change up and add on to in order to suit any occasion. Many of my clients have told me they never knew what to wear to look good for casual events, such as running errands, meeting up with friends, or going on a daytime date. Silhouette outfits have become the ideal way for them to create comfortable, stylish outfits that make them feel confident for the everyday moments of their lives.

For casual silhouettes, you can use the same garments you use for work, but you may want to invest in different fabrics that will transform the look and feeling of your casual clothes. Your everyday silhouettes can range from elegant to casual to athletic. Fabrics that work well are stretch cottons, techno blends, modal blends, ribbed knits, denims, and stretch rayons.

While your casual clothes are primarily reserved for your leisure time, they can easily cross over to a casual work environment. You can even make a comfortable and chic pair of pajamas using the silhouettes. Use a lightweight pull-on palazzo pant with a loose-fitting, soft tank top, and you have a set of indoor loungewear that you can wear outside, too!

For a casual hangout, slip on a pair of black or dark-wash straight-leg jeans and match them with a T-shirt or a turtleneck. Finish with a ballet flat or a kitten heel pump.

dressy silhouette outfits

Whether you need the perfect upscale look for a gala, a killer combination for a special party, or a snazzy ensemble for an evening wedding, the silhouettes can help you deliver that instant "wow" factor. Not only will you look stunning and feel comfortable, but putting together your look will be a breeze!

This is your chance to reach for the ultimate neckline and utilize dressy fabrics, such as silk, satin, velvet, chiffon, and sequins. If you are on a budget, simply utilize your upscale silhouettes from your work wardrobe. No one will know the difference. (I do it all the time!) My go-to silhouettes for dressy events are made of matte stretch knit jersey, and I wear them for work and casual events as well. To create a formal silhouette, I change up my shoes and personality pieces. For example, a pair of stiletto heels or strappy sandals and chandelier earrings add instant red-carpet glamour!

For a dressy event, try pairing a mermaid-style maxi skirt with a spaghetti-strap silk charmeuse tank and a strappy high-heeled sandal. Or start with chiffon palazzo pants, add a beaded tank or an ultimate neckline, and finish with a stiletto ankle boot for lift.

More Examples for Dressy Occasions

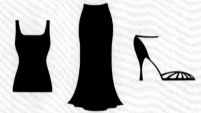

- Dressy Tank
- Dressy Maxi Skirt
- Heeled Strappy Sandal

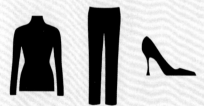

- Dressy Turtleneck
- Dressy Straight-Leg Pant
- Pump

CLIENT CONFESSIONS

Cathy Takes a Trip

Now that you've seen how simple it is to put together attractive silhouette outfits, let me tell you about how I used the Silhouette Solution to solve an everyday wardrobe dilemma. Cathy, a client of mine, recently called me with a fashion emergency. She was leaving for a three-week trip that would involve business meetings, professional workshops, and a vacation.

She was trying to figure out what to pack to meet all of her needs and felt confused. *How could she have the outfits she needed for all her events without packing her entire closet?* Lucky for her, the Silhouette Solution is designed for this exact situation.

We began by selecting complete silhouette outfits. For the colder weather of New York, we selected a set of black silhouettes: a straight-leg pant, a tank top (for layering), a turtleneck, and flat ankle boots for meetings and walking around New York City. For evening events and dinners, we added a pencil skirt, an ultimate neckline, and elegant block heel suede pumps. For the second leg of her trip—a writer's workshop and vacation in Hawaii—we needed clothes for a warmer and more relaxed climate. We selected white linen wide-leg pants, a tank top and a T-shirt, and a white maxi skirt. Then we chose simple yet elegant flat metallic gold sandals and flip-flops for casual wear.

Within minutes, we had put together three weeks' worth of outfits for any occasion that might arise. Cathy didn't have to pack half her wardrobe or carry multiple suitcases. In fact, her three-week wardrobe fit easily into one checked suitcase. By mixing and matching her silhouette garments and personality pieces, we created a variety of stunning outfits to fit any occasion. While you may not be packing for a three-week trip, if the Silhouette Solution can solve this fashion emergency, imagine how it can improve your morning!

office to evening

To turn a workday silhouette into an evening outfit, simply change into a more upscale flat or a heel. For example, you may go from the ballet flat to a strappy open-toe or closed-toe high-heeled sandal with subtle embellishment. And if you choose to wear flats, transition from a daytime leather or suede ballet flat to an evening satin, sequin, or velvet style.

creating exciting silhouette outfits

There are endless possibilities when it comes to building your silhouette outfit using the carefully curated tops, bottoms, and shoes I have selected for the system. And what bliss there is in knowing that whatever you need for any type of event, whether planned or last minute, is hanging elegantly in your closet, just waiting to be debuted.

In the next chapter, I'll show you how to infuse your unique personality into the Silhouette Solution system and help you discover how to express your authentic style with grace and elegance using specific garments. These "personality pieces," as I fondly refer to them, are designed to enhance the basic silhouettes and allow you to change up your look for any event in your life, whether a garden party or a gala. Dressing has never been so easy!

Style is something each of
us already has, all we need
to do is find it.
–DIANE VON FURSTENBERG

personality
pieces

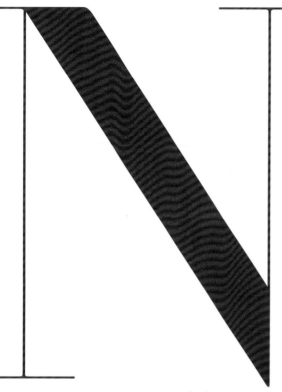

OW IS WHEN OUR ADVENTURE REALLY picks up speed and allows you to exercise your own creativity and fashion sense. You've already discovered how the foundational garments of the Silhouette Solution combine to create 96 outfits; next, I'll let you in on the secret to expanding your possibilities and making these elegant and functional outfits shine! In this chapter, you will learn about the amazing world of personality pieces—the garments and accessories you can add to your silhouettes to create beautiful outfits and distinguish your look.

Imagine walking into a closet filled with clothes and accessories that you adore and that all feel like "you." I will show you how to do it! Meet three women from different walks of life who are happily living out their style:

RACHEL is a young professional who works in an office in the city and who is looking to make her way up the corporate ladder. Her daily work attire consists of an elegant straight-leg dress pant, a tank, a blouse, and a well-cut jacket. She accessorizes with understated jewelry and an attractive heel or pointed-toe flat. Even when she's not at the office, Rachel loves wearing classic styles, such as straight-leg dark jeans, colorful V-neck sweaters, and crisp button-down shirts.

CLAIRE is a dance teacher who loves bright colors, prints, and embellishments, like beading and fringe. She gravitates toward comfortable, flowy silhouettes like palazzo pants and loose tunic-length tanks to allow for maximum movement. She's a free spirit who often receives compliments on her eclectic fashion choices.

SONYA is an advertising executive whose job requires her to travel globally and conduct business in a variety of environments. For presentations and meetings, her uniform of choice is an elegant power jacket, a knee-length pencil skirt, and a formfitting tank, paired with some refined statement jewelry or a scarf. She finishes her look with a pair of sophisticated stiletto heels to give her petite frame a lift. She enjoys utilizing her collection of tailored jackets and feels confident whether she's headed to a business lunch or into the boardroom.

If you lined up Rachel, Claire, and Sonya, you would see that they look quite different from one another, yet each is equally stunning in her own way. The important thing they have in common, however, is that they all use the Silhouette Solution system. What makes these three ladies each look brilliant and unique is their choice of what I call "personality pieces."

Your foundational silhouette outfits—the top, bottom, and shoes—set the groundwork of your wardrobe. The personality pieces—which include jackets (long, short, or cropped), blouses, cardigans, vests, dusters, hats, jewelry, scarves, and other accessories—allow you to express your own individual style. They also make updating your wardrobe a breeze. As you train your eye to choose modern and timeless pieces, you can simply add new or different personality pieces to your silhouettes each season to easily expand your wardrobe.

Personality pieces are the garments and accessories you layer over your basic silhouette outfit to create endless options and express your individual style. Some women love to wear a plain silhouette outfit; in fact, I often do! But in this chapter, I am going to help you determine the personality pieces that will make you look and feel like your best and brightest self. Without further ado, let me give you a quick introduction to some of my favorite universally flattering, elegant, and versatile personality pieces.

meet the
personality pieces

Here are the 24 items that make up the personality pieces in the Silhouette Solution. Don't feel like you need to buy all of them. Instead, choose as many or as few as you'd like. The goal here is to express your personal style, which you'll learn more about on page 131. Then you'll see these pieces again as part of complete outfits in chapters 7, 8, and 9.

FOR THE WORKPLACE

Black Blazer

Colored Jacket

White Shirt

Silk Charmeuse Blouse

Open-Front Drape Cardigan

Classic Cardigan

Perfect Jewelry

Trench Coat

FOR CASUAL EVENTS

Athletic Jacket

Denim Jacket

Leather Jacket

V-Neck Sweater

Vest

Caftan

Hoodie

Duster

FOR DRESSY OCCASIONS

Evening Wrap

Glitzy Evening Jacket

Shrug

Organza Blouse or Jacket

Statement Necklace

Statement Brooch

Chandelier Earrings

Evening Purse

Imagine
walking into
a closet filled
with clothes
and accessories
that you adore
and that all feel
like "you."

choosing the right personality pieces

Whether you are a clothing minimalist or a fashionista, there are some essential guidelines to consider when adding personality pieces to your Silhouette Solution wardrobe. Before I purchase one of these pieces, I ask myself these questions:

- Does the shape and style flatter my body?

- Is the fabric fluid, and does it drape well on my body?

- Does the color flatter my skin tone?

DOES THE SHAPE AND STYLE FLATTER MY BODY?

Regardless of your height or weight, most women want to appear long and lean. The right style will make you look taller and thinner. One technique to achieving this goal is to wear personality pieces that cover the hip, butt, and upper thigh area. These longer garments, which often open in the front, showcase the silhouette and fall anywhere from the upper thigh to the knee. Examples include structured jackets and coats, as well as open-front cardigans and dusters. Traditional fashion rules state that shorter women should avoid these styles, but I'm here to tell you that these ultraflattering garments look fabulous on everyone! I have rarely met a client who hasn't absolutely loved this complimentary style.

IS THE FABRIC FLUID, AND DOES IT DRAPE WELL ON MY BODY?

Fabric choice is important when selecting personality pieces. For the elongated garments I just mentioned, select fabrics that feel "flowy." A fluid fabric drapes comfortably, doesn't cling, and moves with ease. Choose fabrics such as rayon, viscose, or modal that contain a small percentage of spandex (or Lycra) to give them movement. Natural fabrics, such as linen, fine wool, silk, or cotton, also work.

For more tailored garments, such as structured blazers, coats, and jackets, be concerned with fit and form. Choose fabrics that have a luxurious feeling next to your skin and that slim the look of your body. With the wide variety of options available today, you can choose a high-quality synthetic blend of modal and cotton, wool, or silk, or natural fabrics such as pure cotton or wool.

DOES THE COLOR FLATTER MY SKIN TONE?

Personality pieces offer you the opportunity to add a kaleidoscope of colors to your wardrobe. Maybe you have been told, "That color looks great on you!" I'm sure you walked a little taller after receiving such a compliment. Wearing the right colors is essential to creating an appealing and empowering personal appearance.

The trick to using color successfully is to wear shades that harmonize with your natural skin tone and features—something I will show you how to do. When you wear the correct colors, in the correct tones—light or dark, soft or bright, warm or cool—your natural beauty emerges, and your appearance seems to magically transform. You will look younger, healthier, and more vibrant—all from wearing colors that boost your natural beauty!

Marina Tries Something Different

My client stands 5-feet-3-inches tall and is full-figured. For years, she followed conventional fashion advice that cautioned her against wearing a long jacket or an open-front cardigan, because these garments would "swallow" her or make her appear shorter or wider.

When I urged her to try these personality pieces, she discovered that they actually did the opposite. Partnered with a comfortable silhouette outfit of wide-leg pants, an elongated tunic-length tank top, and a heeled ankle boot or sandal, she not only looked taller and slimmer, but she also felt more comfortable and attractive.

color tone exercise

At the beginning of nearly every color consultation I give, clients invariably tell me about all the colors they have decided they like or dislike, and those they can and cannot wear. I gently encourage them to consider that their perceptions may not be entirely accurate. The following exercise will help you discover the colors that are most flattering to you. I encourage you to trust the process, as the results are often illuminating. Keep this guiding principle in mind: *It's never about the actual color; it's about the effect the color has on your skin.*

What I mean by this is that, in order to look your best, your color selections should never be based on whether you like or dislike the color, but on how the color affects and alters your appearance.

HOW TO CHOOSE YOUR BEST COLORS

- Go into your wardrobe and select two different colored tops to compare with each other next to your skin. Leave them on the hangers. The garment could be a jacket, a shirt, or a blouse. If possible, try to compare two different shades of the same color—for example, bright white and off-white, or deep red and bright red. Comparing two different colors is also fine.

- Take your choices to a mirror (natural lighting is best). You don't need a full-length mirror, but you should be able to see your face and neck clearly. Pull your hair back into a ponytail or a bun so that you can focus on your face and remove any makeup you're wearing to reveal your natural coloring.

- Hold the two garments, one behind the other, under your chin.

- Close your eyes and take a deep breath. Open your eyes and look at your face in the mirror. It's important that you do not look at the garment. Look to see how the color of the garment affects and alters the appearance of your skin and facial features. Remember, it's not about the color, it's about how the color affects your skin.

- With your left hand, remove the top garment from under your chin. Wait a moment. Then look at your face with the second garment under your chin. What differences do you notice? Does your skin appear darker or lighter? Do different highlights appear? Now go back to the first garment.

- Go back and forth between the garments a few times. Concentrate on your face and notice the changes. Does your under-eye area look darker with one than with the other? Do any blemishes or marks on your face become more prominent with one than the other? Does the overall appearance of your skin look clearer, smoother, and more vibrant with one compared to the other? Does one color cast more shadows on your face compared to the other? Does your face and neck area appear heavier with one color compared to the other?

- Return to your closet and repeat this exercise with other selections, making note of the ones that flatter and enliven your face the most.

How eye-opening was this exercise for you? Wearing the right tone or shade of color will always give your skin a healthy glow. Maybe you love the look of a crisp white shirt, but ivory is the shade that brightens and warms up your face.

Try this fun exercise. Next time you are watching an awards ceremony on television, look closely at the actresses walking on the red carpet. What do you see first? The dress or the woman? If it's the dress, you can be sure they are wearing the wrong color!

Identifying a few flattering colors in your own closet is a great way to begin your color-finding adventure. Be willing to engage with color and give it a chance! There are many colors that, at one time, I never would have considered wearing. But today, they fill my wardrobe because I know that when I wear them, I will look powerful, captivating, and confident. And yes, I do give myself permission to look powerful, captivating, and confident. You can, too!

finding
your style

Before you go shopping, there is one more all-important question you must ask: What is my style? Remember Rachel, Claire, and Sonya—the young professional, the dance teacher, and the advertising executive? Each woman has a different work environment, lifestyle, and personality. Claire gravitates toward large jewelry, bright colors, and floppy hats, while Sonya prefers power jackets, quality fabrics, and statement pieces. And Rachel is drawn to a more traditional look, such as straight-leg jeans, V-neck sweaters, and crisp button-down shirts.

Think about yourself for a minute. Do you like dressing in a casual or a dramatic way? Conservative or artistic? Traditional or romantic? The combination of your chosen silhouettes plus your personality pieces determines your style. To feel truly authentic and at ease in your clothes, you must discover who *you* are.

Before adding personality pieces to your wardrobe, ask yourself: What style of clothing makes me feel my most confident, comfortable, and attractive? I call this your "style ID." Your clothes communicate so much about you before you even say hello. If you're unsure of your style ID, you may feel uncomfortable with your clothing choices.

> Your clothes communicate so much about you before you even say hello.

find your style ID
exercise

I've outlined eight different style IDs below. To determine your style ID, read through each list of words and think about your own personality, lifestyle, and daily environments. Focus on the essence of who you truly are—for example, free-spirited, traditional, whimsical, nonconformist—versus who you wish you were. Note your first, second, and third choices.

1. Take three deep breaths to relax and center yourself.

2. Slowly and thoughtfully read the following eight style ID descriptions. After reading them through twice, mark your top three choices in pencil.

   _____ A. Structured, tailored, conventional, appropriate, practical, unadorned, sensible

   _____ B. Chic, contemporary, cutting edge, modern, popular

   _____ C. Classy, upscale, sophisticated, polished, stylish, refined, timeless

   _____ D. Simple, streamlined, neutral, uncluttered, clean

   _____ E. Poetic, lyrical, soft, beautiful, flowery, feminine, delicate, sensual

   _____ F. Active, informal, relaxed, sporty, versatile, lightweight, breathable

   _____ G. Exciting, mysterious, alluring, enchanting, charismatic, engaging, captivating

   _____ H. Free-spirited, individualist, artistic, creative, nonconformist

3. After you have read each list of words a few times, pause to think about how each list resonates with you.

4. Pay attention to how each grouping of words makes you *feel* as you read and notice any emotions that arise. Observe if you feel a connection to one or two lists more than the others. If you looked at one of the lists and said, "Ah! That's me!" congratulations, you've discovered your style ID! Maybe you found that you are a combination of two or more style types. Many people are a combination of two or three styles.

5. Take note of the top three lists that resonate with you the most. Now look at the answers to reveal what style ID you chose!

ANSWERS

A. The Traditionalist	E. The Romantic
B. The Trendsetter	F. The Casual Athlete
C. The Elegant Sophisticate	G. The Glamourista
D. The Minimalist	H. The Bohemian

Of the eight style ID types, which one or two resonated with you the most? You may like to wear one style at work and enjoy another style at home. While I dabble in all of the style IDs at times, I am a combination of the Elegant Sophisticate and the Bohemian. Still feel uncertain about your style? That's okay! As you learn the Silhouette Solution system, you will be able to experiment with different personality pieces to hone your style.

Don't be alarmed if your preferred style ID doesn't seem like a fit for your chosen profession—for example, you are a business executive who chose Romantic or Bohemian. Using the sophisticated foundation of the silhouettes, you can add subtle personality pieces that are appropriate and attractive for work but still convey the spirit of your style.

When a woman connects to one of the eight style IDs, it gives her confidence to see, accept, and express her unique beauty and style.

the great eight style IDs

Now, let's take a closer look at the eight style IDs. These eight style personalities are some of my go-to favorites when I work with clients. In my experience, when a woman connects to one of the eight style IDs, it gives her confidence to see, accept, and express her unique beauty and style.

Keep in mind that these are my top eight style IDs and are certainly not every possible style. If you don't connect with any of them, that's okay. But I do want you to explore and experiment to find the style ID—or combination of IDs—that fits you the best. These eight style IDs, while different from one another, also share something in common: each can be expressed easily in a way that is modern, flattering, and elegant, and their correlating garments can be found in stores every season. You can also combine these IDs to create hundreds of modern, stylish looks.

All eight are versatile and transition easily from the workplace to dressy occasions to everyday life. A client once told me that the moment she connected to her style ID, she felt like she had come home to herself. She became more accepting of herself and felt more at ease and confident in her body. That's how I want you to *always* feel!

The Traditionalist

- STRUCTURED
- TAILORED
- CONVENTIONAL
- APPROPRIATE
- PRACTICAL
- UNADORNED
- SENSIBLE

The traditionalist look is elegant, unpretentious, and well-tailored. Traditional style avoids garments that are loud or attract attention, such as bold colors, prints, or dramatic jewelry. This wardrobe consists of beautiful basics such as pencil skirts, solid blouses, crisp button-down shirts, and structured blazers. The classic cardigan and a trench coat are staple personality pieces of the traditionalist style.

Rather than following trends, the traditionalist style ID favors tradition and does not include clothes that are flashy, avant-garde, or overly dramatic. If you do want to jazz up this look and add a touch of sex appeal, wear a stiletto heel.

The Trendsetter

- CHIC
- CONTEMPORARY
- CUTTING EDGE
- MODERN
- POPULAR

The trendsetter expresses the most recent fashions and ideas in the way she adapts her silhouettes. She is modern and loves incorporating the hottest trends. Each season she experiences joy and fulfillment from changing up her style with modern colors, shapes, and accessories over her silhouettes.

This style ID is hard to categorize, as its identity is constantly in motion, changing with the trends. However, here is an example of how a trendsetter might update her wardrobe: If Bermuda shorts, bright neon colors, and crochet dresses were the hot looks of the season, a trendsetter might throw a crochet duster over her silhouette outfit, opt for a pair of classy black Bermuda shorts instead of a pencil skirt, or wear an eye-catching neon pink trench coat for an up-to-the-minute look. Her eight great shoes may also reflect the latest styles.

The Elegant Sophisticate

- CLASSY
- UPSCALE
- SOPHISTICATED
- POLISHED
- STYLISH
- REFINED
- TIMELESS

The elegant sophisticate exemplifies grace, refinement, and good taste. The sophisticate's style screams quality, even if she purchased her clothes at a bargain. This style ID is recognizable by its clean lines and classic colors.

The elegant sophisticate invests in upscale accessories such as statement jewelry, silk print scarves, and chic handbags. She loves structured personality pieces such as jackets (long or short) in rich fabrics like leather, velvet, and gabardine. She may be spotted wearing an elegant animal print silk charmeuse blouse with an exquisitely tailored suit and black suede heels or dark wash jeans with a turtleneck, suede stiletto ankle boots, and a soft leather jacket. The elegant sophisticate knows how to navigate the trends and make thoughtful selections that transcend time so that she can wear them for many seasons and make a lasting and refined statement.

The Minimalist

- SIMPLE
- STREAMLINED
- UNCLUTTERED
- NEUTRAL
- CLEAN

Minimalist style is defined by one principle: Keep it simple! The minimalist embraces such style through a modern, unembellished, and streamlined look. Her style involves minimal prints; basic, clean lines; and high-quality fabrics. The minimalist prefers natural fabrics, such as cotton, wool, linen, and silk. Although the minimalist style ID is unadorned, that doesn't mean she has to live in a world of basic colors. She loves rocking neutrals as well as pops of her favorite hues in her personality pieces.

The minimalist curates her wardrobe and style with great care, making sure she truly loves each piece. Personality pieces may include a boyfriend cardigan (in several colors), a stunning overcoat, a well-cut blazer, and a colorful scarf.

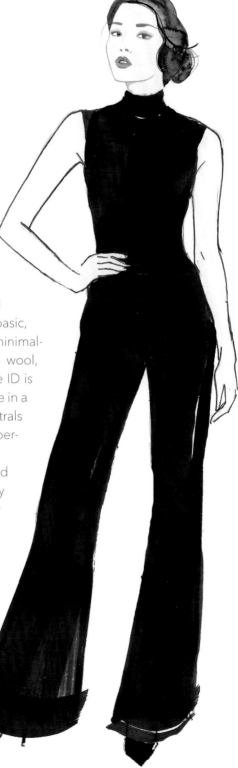

The Romantic

- POETIC
- LYRICAL
- SOFT
- BEAUTIFUL
- FLOWERY
- FEMININE
- DELICATE
- SENSUAL

Romantic style speaks the language of softness and femininity. The romantic dresser gives a nod to the history and enchantment of bygone eras, such as Victorian England. Light and airy fabrics, lace, ruffles, and bows are all staples of the romantic's wardrobe.

The romantic's closet may showcase soft floral blouses with pintuck details, cotton puffed-sleeve shirts, long lace dusters, and delicate chiffon scarves. On the jewelry front, lockets, charm bracelets, and brooches all exemplify the romantic style ID.

The
Casual Athlete

- ACTIVE
- INFORMAL
- RELAXED
- SPORTY
- VERSATILE
- LIGHTWEIGHT
- BREATHABLE

The casual athlete wears practical, sports-inspired clothing that can double as stylish street wear. This style ID is perfect for the woman who enjoys an active lifestyle. The garments in the athletic style are also known as athleisure and consist of clothes that are comfortable, lightweight, and breathable.

This wardrobe consists of both loose-fitting and body-contouring performance fabrics, colorful athletic-fit pants and jackets, polo shirts, and athletic wear separates. In winter, you may see the casual athlete wearing puffer jackets, cozy hoodies, and down-filled vests. This style ID may keep leggings as an alternate part of her wardrobe in addition to straight-leg pull-on athletic pants. And, of course, the stylish sneaker is a must to finish this look.

The Glamourista

- EXCITING
- CHARISMATIC
- MYSTERIOUS
- ENGAGING
- ALLURING
- CAPTIVATING
- ENCHANTING

The glamourista style ID is all about making an impression. Her style is elegant and sexy. Whether she's wearing jeans or an evening gown, she's confident and knows how to play up her assets.

This style ID is dramatic and defined by quality, polished, and luxurious details. The glamourista's closet might contain a mermaid maxi skirt, embellished tank top or jacket, and stiletto heels. A pair of chic dark sunglasses is a staple, as are a statement purse and some luxurious scarves.

The Bohemian

- FREE-SPIRITED
- INDIVIDUALIST
- NONCONFORMIST
- CREATIVE
- ARTISTIC

The bohemian style ID, often referred to in fashion as "boho" or "boho-chic," is all about freedom, harmony, and individuality. The bohemian is creative, free-spirited, and marches to the beat of her own drum. She expresses these characteristics through an eclectic, creative mix of garments and accessories.

Her wardrobe will include worn-in blue jeans, flared pants, vintage jackets, airy tunic-style caftans, and fringe vests. The bohemian wears mixed prints and fabrics with embellishments, such as embroidery, crochet, and beading. When it comes to accessories, the boho woman embraces wide-brim floppy hats, hip belts, kimono-style duster coats, and lots of jewelry.

expressing your style ID

Once you have determined which one or two of the style IDs resonate most with you, begin to notice these looks in the real world. Go online and research the looks you're drawn to. Flip through catalogs and magazines, and pay attention to which outfits excite you the most.

The beauty of these eight style IDs is their versatility. Dress them up or down according to the occasion. Go all out with personality pieces and accessories, or simply add a hint of your style ID with a single piece of jewelry.

Personality pieces are the secret to creating your individual style and filling your wardrobe with clothes and accessories you love. Invest some time into thinking about how you want to look and feel. Once you have discovered the style ID that excites you, gives you confidence, and show-cases your personality, you will be able to create dozens of gorgeous outfits simply by adding your favorite personality pieces to your silhouettes. And you will have a closet filled with clothes that you totally adore!

In the next three chapters, I will share 24 curated fashion formulas that can be adapted to any style ID. Combining the foundational silhouettes with some of my favorite personality pieces will give you exciting outfit options for the workplace, your everyday activities, and special events.

We will begin in the workplace. Using eight personality pieces, I will show you how to dress for work—or for working from home—in a way that makes you feel comfortable, confident, and inspired. When your outfit comes together easily, you can focus on the things that really matter in your workplace.

Personality pieces are the secret to creating your individual style and filling your wardrobe with clothes and accessories you love.

Clothes are the way you present yourself to the world; they affect the way the world feels and thinks about you; subconsciously they affect the way you feel and think about yourself.

—EDITH HEAD

dressing for the nine-to-five

W

HEN I MET JUNE, SHE HAD JUST received a well-deserved pro- motion at the prominent toy manufacturer where she worked. She would be moving into an executive role, where she would be interacting with personnel and VIP clients. Although June was a diligent worker who was excellent at her desk job, she lacked the confidence to dress for her new position, which would put her in front of people on a regular basis.

My goal was to align her appearance with her high level of expertise so that others would view her as an authority and credible in her new role. While June was exceedingly qualified for her new posi- tion, she was a quiet, behind-the-scenes type who liked to focus on her work. She paid little attention to her wardrobe, dressed to blend in as much as possible, and wore clothes that did not truly fit or flatter her body.

As soon as we started to build the foundational silhouettes that complemented her body, and to add appropriate personality pieces, June's posture transformed. She stood taller and rolled her shoulders back in confidence. As we created multiple outfits, June was wowed by her reflection. "I never realized I could look this good!" she said. The Silhouette Solution allowed June to step into her magnificence—and her new position—with confidence and style.

We've all heard it said that you should dress for the job you want. That is absolutely true! I believe it is equally important to dress for your current job in a way that expresses your individual style.

Today, more than ever, we have a wide range of options when it comes to what's acceptable to wear on the job. But dull, ill-fitting, or unflattering garments should never be among them. Instead, you want to present an image of credibility, authority, and integrity, which can elevate the opportunities and possibilities in your career.

In this chapter, I will show you how to coordinate comfortable, stylish career outfits, whether you work in a corporate environment, a creative space, or a home office. Using eight mistake-proof formulas, I'll demonstrate how to combine the silhouettes with my favorite personality pieces to create simple and stylish outfits for work that empower you and allow you to express yourself.

Today, more than ever, we have a wide range of options when it comes to what's acceptable to wear on the job. But dull, ill-fitting or unflattering garments should never be among them.

do me a favor

As you read this chapter, you may encounter some personality pieces that you have never tried. You may think these garments will not look good on you. You may even say, "I can't wear that. It's not my style."

Expecting you to try something outside of your comfort zone (especially when we haven't even met!) is a lot to ask. Trying something new requires courage, openness, and trust. Time and again, I have surprised my clients by suggesting they try on garments they were certain would not work for them. But after they tried the items on, they were shocked to discover how much they loved their new look.

As you read through the formulas, keep an open mind. Doing this may unlock a whole new world of style possibilities, as it has for so many of the people I have worked with.

the great eight formulas for work

These personality pieces are on my favorites list because they are elegant, versatile, universally flattering, and adaptable to any style ID. These ready-to-go looks send a message of credibility, allowing you to walk out the door—or into your home office—with confidence and style.

THE Black Blazer

A beautifully tailored black jacket (also known as a blazer) with a defined shoulder line adds instant authority and sophistication to your look, making it perfect for the workplace. The superpower of this classic personality piece is its ability to cross the divide from formal to casual and embody any of the style IDs. Black jackets come in many different styles, including traditional hip length, cropped (for a less formal look), and long, falling to mid-thigh or even the knee. It's a go-to work piece that easily transitions from the office to an evening event by adding dressier shoes, jewelry, and a small clutch bag.

MONEY-SAVING TIP • To expand your outfit options on a budget, buy a two-piece black suit with either a straight-leg pant or a pencil skirt (or both). Those who wear a suit for work can also separate the pieces, using the bottom as a silhouette piece and the jacket as a personality piece for other outfits.

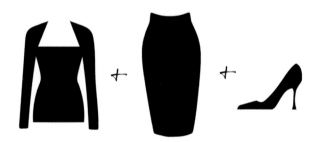

Formula # 1

The Black Blazer

The Ultimate Neckline

The Pencil Skirt

The Pump

Formula # 2

The Turtleneck

The White Shirt

The Wide-wLeg Pant

The Heeled Ankle Boot

THE White Shirt

A white button-up shirt is fresh, crisp, and classic. This versatile garment brings polish and professionalism to your work attire. Keep it simple with a traditional button-up front, a classic collar, and cuffs. Or, for a more bohemian or romantic vibe, add a little flair with a ruffled front or ruffled cuffs. I love to use an oversize white button-up as an open-front overshirt with the tank, straight-leg pants, and heeled ankle boots. The white button-up also pairs beautifully with the black or colored blazer.

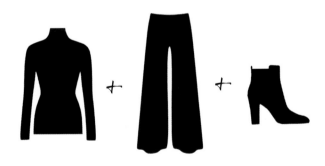

THE Colored Blazer

A colored jacket or blazer adds a lively, sophisticated vibe to your look. (To find your winning colors, refer to the exercise on page 129.) Start with a pair of straight-leg pants and a T-shirt (or a flounced pencil skirt and a tank) and add a tailored jacket and some jewelry for an eye-catching look. For a more casual dress code, combine your favorite colored jacket with a pair of jeans and a flat or heeled shoe for a look that's perfect for meeting friends for happy hour.

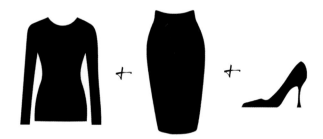

The Colored Blazer

The T-Shirt

The Pencil Skirt

The Pump

Formula # 4

The
Silk Charmeuse
Blouse

The
Tank

The
Wide-Leg
Pant

The
Pump

THE Silk Charmeuse Blouse

A silk charmeuse blouse adds a touch of sophisticated glamour. This blouse is available in a variety of styles and sleeve lengths. My favorites are the classic silk shirt style with a collar and cuffs, or one that features a bow at the neck and a fuller sleeve. Wear this upscale piece with blue jeans, black suede pumps, or ankle boots for a casual working environment. It also transitions perfectly from day to evening.

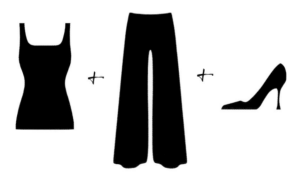

THE Open-Front Drape Cardigan

The open-front drape cardigan is perfect for more casual workplaces. Less formal than the structured jacket but not as relaxed as a knit cardigan, this personality piece is fluid and flattering. Unlike a traditional knit cardigan, it is usually made of a soft lightweight jersey knit without buttons or closures. This elegant personality piece can easily transition to weekends. For a bohemian look, pair it with a belt worn at the hips and a small neck scarf or long necklace. This modern and chic garment lengthens the body, making you appear long and lean.

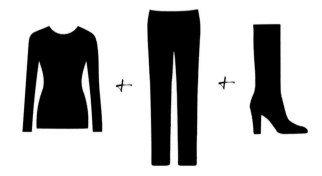

Formula # 5

The T-Shirt

The Open-Front
Drape Cardigan

The
Straight-Leg
Pant

The
Heeled
Knee Boot

Formula # 6

The
Classic
Cardigan

The Tank

The
Flounced
Pencil Skirt

The
Ballet Flat

THE Classic Cardigan

Elegant and relaxed, a classic cardigan in a fine knit fabric provides an informal yet put-together look for work. This classic cardigan hits at the waist or just below it and can be worn open or buttoned. It looks amazing with simple touches, such as a pearl necklace or a silver bracelet. For a conservative look, wear it over a white button-up shirt. The classic cardigan is also a great finishing touch for any of the sleeveless Silhouette Solution tops or dresses.

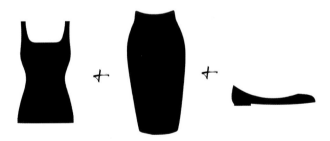

THE Perfect Jewelry

Whether discreet or dramatic, jewelry adds interest and makes a basic outfit look polished. For the woman who prefers wearing simple basics to work, jewelry is the perfect accessory. To create a harmonious look, choose a theme, such as gold, silver, pearls, or gemstones—and be consistent. Think about what pairs well with your style ID—sophisticated, bohemian, minimalist, or glamorous.

To add some chic adornment to a simple outfit, I layer necklaces of different lengths. I'll pair a 36-inch seed pearl necklace with a shorter 13-inch fine gold chain and pendant. Or I'll wear one bold pendant on a mid-length chain for a more dramatic effect. While not exactly jewelry, a gold Chanel-style chain belt worn at the hip or just below the waist dresses up a simple pencil skirt.

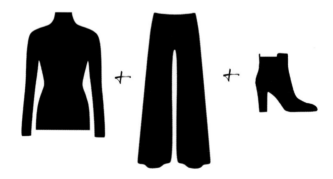

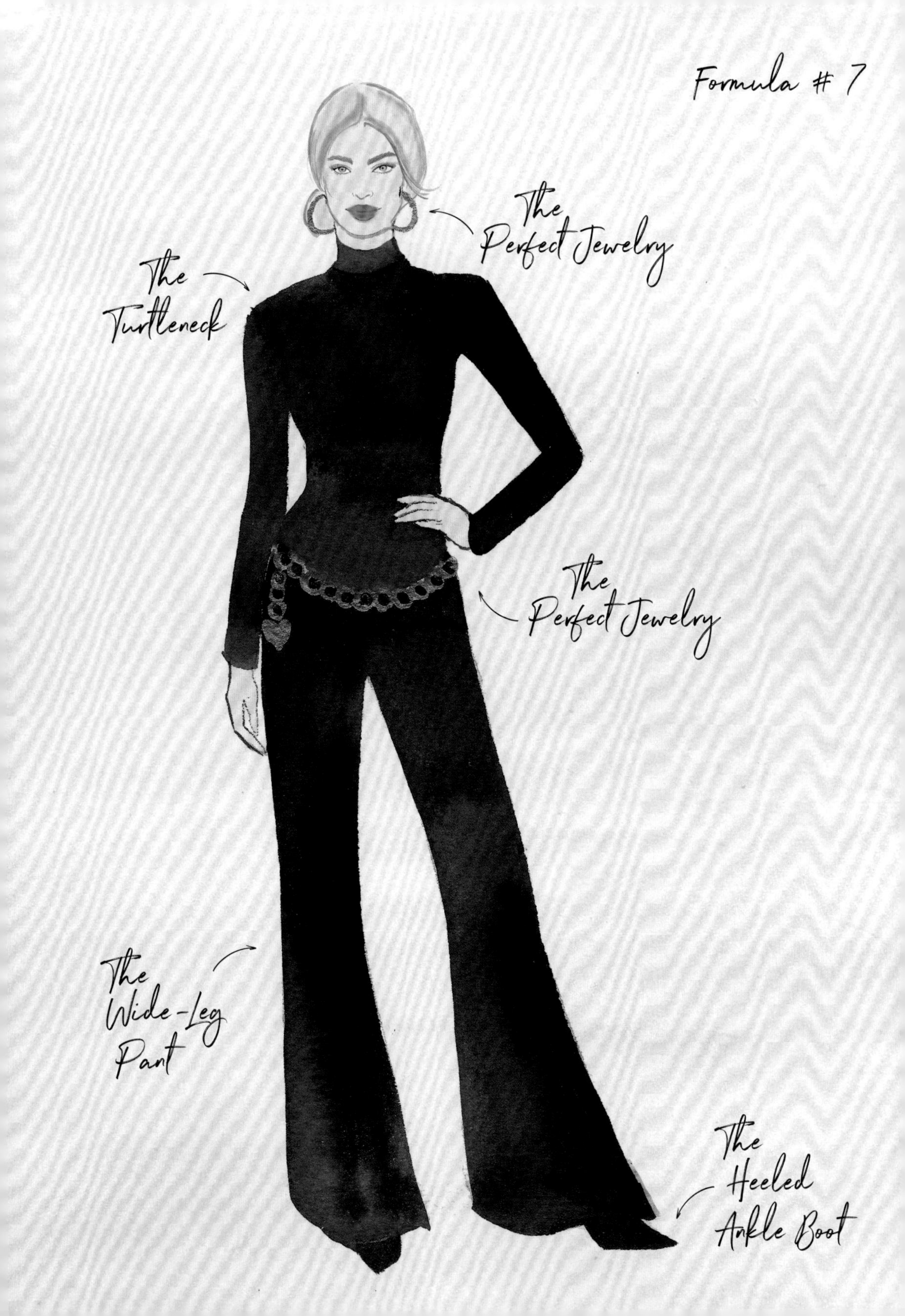

Formula # 7

The
Perfect Jewelry

The
Turtleneck

The
Perfect Jewelry

The
Wide-Leg
Pant

The
Heeled
Ankle Boot

Formula # 8

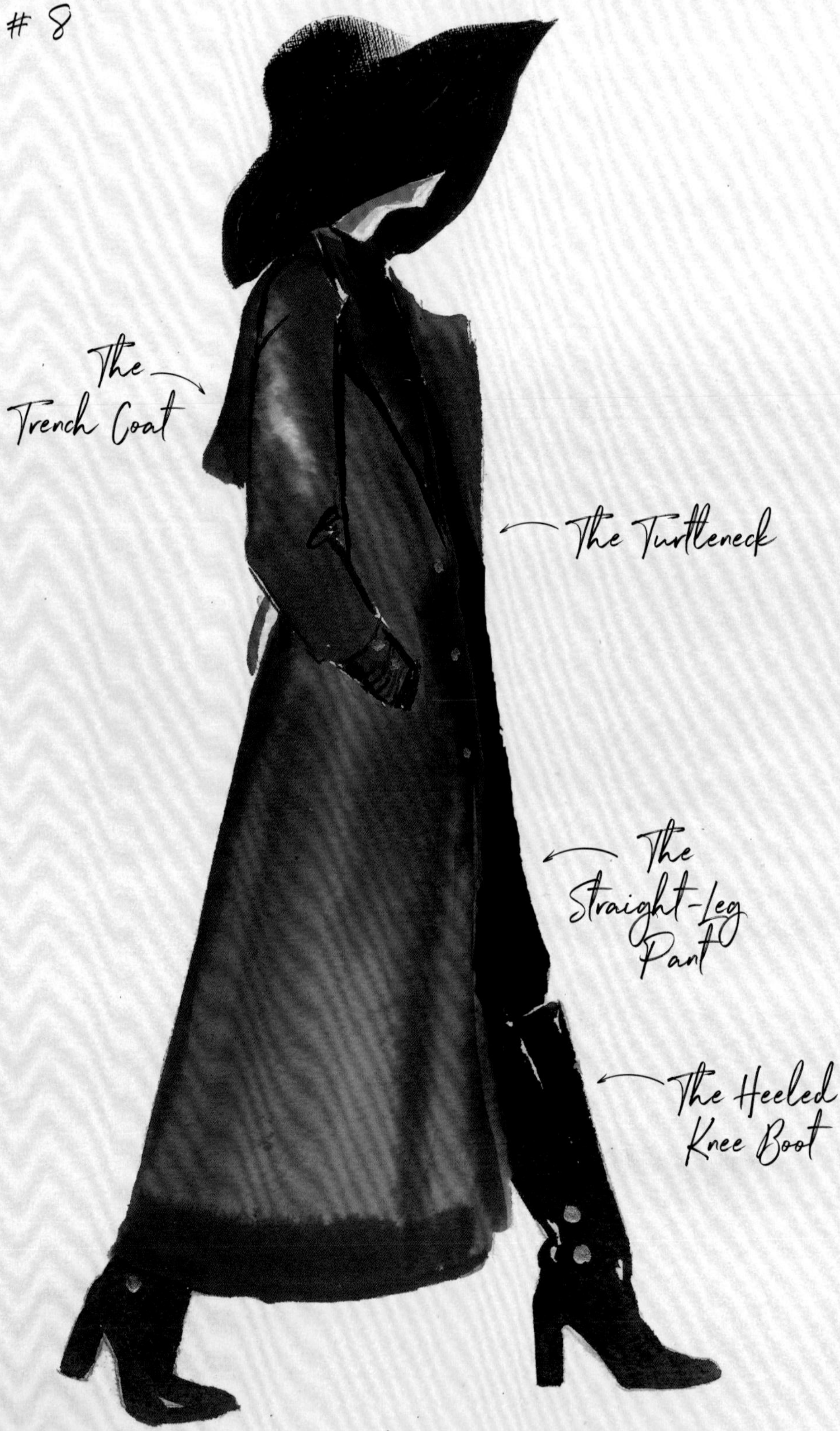

The
Trench Coat

The Turtleneck

The
Straight-Leg
Pant

The Heeled
Knee Boot

THE Trench Coat

During the past century, this iconic coat has become a fashion staple for both men and women. Wear this classic item over any silhouette outfit to look authoritative, chic, and put together. The classic trench offers light warmth and protection from rain during the spring and fall or year-round in mild climates. Wear it over straight-leg pants or jeans with a ballet flat, or over a pencil skirt with heels. This coat is so sophisticated and so versatile! Tie your look together with a floral or printed scarf, and you're ready for work.

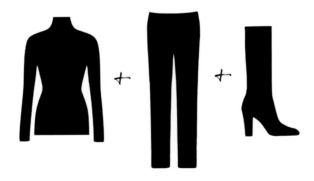

CLIENT CONFESSIONS

Michelle dresses for her home office

Michelle, a mom who transitioned her career from a corporate setting to working from home, found herself in a major style slump and a little depressed. No longer needing to choose professional office wear, she usually spent her workday in sweats or pajamas. When she was interacting with clients over the phone (even if they could not see her), she felt she'd lost the bold, assertive edge she'd had in the workplace.

Michelle wanted to know what she could wear during the day to feel comfortable *and* professional, without putting on a business suit or high heels. I suggested several options: a navy or black silhouette outfit with a stretch pull-on straight-leg pant, a short-sleeve or long-sleeve T-shirt, and a ballet flat. For video conferences or meetings outside the home, I suggested a pencil skirt with a wide strap tank, an open-front cardigan or soft jacket, and ankle boots. I showed Michelle how to combine any of the silhouette pieces to create attractive and appropriate outfits.

Once she was able to put together simple, stylish work-from-home outfits, Michelle discovered that what you wear not only affects your appearance but also affects your behavior. Michelle's new wardrobe motivated her to accomplish her professional goals, increasing her productivity and enhancing her sense of well-being. She now leaves the sweats and T-shirts for the weekend and puts together a stylish Silhouette Solution outfit before walking into her home office.

make a dramatic transformation

On page 119, I showed you how to easily transition from work to after-work activities by simply changing your shoes. But by using a few personality pieces, you can make an even more fabulous transformation.

1. Transition tote—In my car I like to keep a tote bag that holds a pair of shoes, some jewelry (in a sheer drawstring organza bag), some extra makeup, and a few scarves and lightweight cardigans. If you don't drive to work, keep a bag like this at your office, allowing you to change up your look at a moment's notice.

2. Shoes—If you know you have an after-work dinner or event, simply pack a dressy pair of pumps or heeled strappy sandals in your tote.

3. An evening purse—If you use a larger purse or tote during the day, be sure to pack an elegant clutch or small purse with a strap to carry along your essential items for the evening.

4. Jewelry—Transition to evening by adding a few dramatic pieces of jewelry, such as chandelier earrings or a statement necklace.

Whether you are conducting meetings face-to-face or through a computer screen, dressing in an appealing, professional way will boost your confidence and help you make a great first impression. Never underestimate the impact of looking and feeling your best.

Now that you know how to put together a great outfit for work, let's turn our attention to your everyday life. I will share eight Silhouette Solution formulas to help you look chic while running errands, going on dates, heading to the gym, or hanging out with friends. Using eight more of my favorite personality pieces and the foundational silhouettes, I will show you how to upgrade your wardrobe—and maybe even your social life. Let's get to it!

Fashion has two purposes:
comfort and love. Beauty
comes when fashion
succeeds.

–COCO CHANEL

dressing for a casual vibe

Y DEAR FRIEND YVONNE, a photographer and an artist, had just about given up on herself. As we chatted over a cup of tea one afternoon, she told me she was falling into the habit of immediately turning down social invitations.

"Brenda," she said, "I'm embarrassed and a little ashamed to tell you this, but I just can't put myself together in a way that makes me feel presentable. It's easier to just stay home." My heart went out to her. We've all experienced those discouraging moments when our inner closet tells us, "You have nothing to wear." I knew my friend just needed some fresh inspiration regarding what to wear to social engagements, such as dinner with friends and art openings.

We opened up her closet. I asked if she had a pair of straight-leg jeans, a tank top, a turtleneck, and a pair of flat ankle boots all in the same color. She rummaged through her belongings and produced exactly what I had asked for. Next, I had her try them on. She looked in the mirror and couldn't believe what she saw.

"Brenda, I love it!" she said. "Why didn't I think of this?" I showed her a few other silhouette alternatives and how she could use personality pieces, such as a pretty cardigan or a chic jacket, to finish her look.

Yvonne had everything she needed right in her closet. Using the Silhouette Solution system, we were able to change Yvonne's perception of herself and reignite her social life in less than ten minutes. She now feels confident about her appearance, enjoys going to dinner with friends, and regularly attends art openings in her community.

the great eight
for the everyday

While it may be tempting to throw on a pair of sweats and a T-shirt when you're not at work or when you're working from home without any scheduled meetings, your clothes say something about you, whether you like it or not. What you put on affects how you think, feel, and behave, which can leave a positive or negative impression on those with whom you interact.

When you give some thought to your appearance—even for those more leisurely times—you may find that your whole demeanor changes. You may even notice that you have better interactions with others. I've watched it happen dozens of times. My client sets aside her sweats, puts on a marvelous Silhouette Solution outfit, and suddenly feels more comfortable in her own skin. People treat her differently because she is confident in who she is, and she radiates that to others!

These eight Silhouette Solution formulas will help you dress for success in your everyday life. Whether you're going to brunch with friends or getting ready for a date, these formulas make it easy to choose an outfit. If you love to wear jeans, casual events are the perfect opportunity to replace your straight-leg pants with a pair of straight-leg jeans.

THE
Athletic
Jacket

Whether or not you're a gym enthusiast, a formfitting athletic jacket is a great piece to create casual, sporty outfits. This jacket looks great over your workout silhouette or with a T-shirt and jeans. Wear it while exercising outdoors or to meet a friend for coffee.

The athletic jacket is a dream for travel, because it doesn't crease or take up a lot of space. Choose a flattering color or a dark tone for a minimalist monochromatic look, and you'll want to wear it everywhere—not just to the gym! Speaking of the gym, exercise is a great way to clear your "inner closet," so allow this breathable beauty to inspire you to get moving.

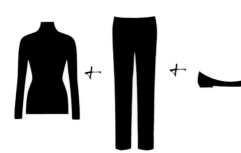

THE
Hoodie

A hoodie is a sporty, comfortable, and cozy addition to your casual wardrobe. Perfect for football games, walking downtown in cooler months, or running to the store, a hoodie is surprisingly versatile and comes in many different styles. Choose one that zips up for a slim-fitting style or a loose pullover variety for something more comfortable and casual. The secret to a fashionable hoodie is choosing a great color with a good fit in a quality fabric.

A hoodie is perfect for wearing around the house, but you can also wear one as part of a cool, casual weekend outfit. Just pair it with the right pieces! For example, wear a colorful hoodie under a leather jacket or coat, with a pair of straight-leg jeans and ankle boots.

THE
Leather Jacket

While a more considered purchase, a lightweight leather jacket is one of the most versatile pieces you can own. High-end and sophisticated, it comes in many flattering styles, from a conservative leather blazer to a Chanel-style quilted biker jacket to a suede moto jacket. Choose a lightweight, soft leather in a vibrant color for warm weather and a heavier weight in a neutral color for the colder months. A suave leather jacket can easily cross over into your work wardrobe, too! Wear it with a turtleneck and one of the fab four bottoms or jeans and ankle boots for a super casual look.

MONEY-SAVING TIP • Faux or vegan leather can achieve the same look, so be willing to explore various fabrics according to your lifestyle preferences and budget.

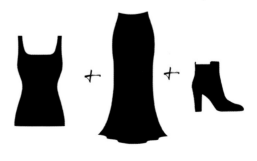

THE
V-Neck Sweater

Talk about a universal crowd-pleaser! A V-neck sweater works wonderfully for the traditionalist and minimalist style IDs, but it can also be styled as part of a soft, romantic, or even bohemian look. V-necks come in many flattering lengths—waist, tunic, cropped, and even dress length. This sweater easily crosses over from work to your casual life, and you can find it in stylish fabrics such as cashmere, wool, or light, luxurious cotton or rayon blends.

My favorite is a long, oversize black V-neck that covers my hips and butt, providing me with that security layer I love. For a sleek effect, try a formfitting, knee-length V-neck sweater dress over straight-leg pants with heeled ankle boots. Add a two-inch-wide hip belt for a little funkiness. Whether you wear a classic trim-and-slim style or layer an oversize V-neck over a white shirt with the tails and cuffs showing, the V-neck is an attractive asset to your casual wardrobe.

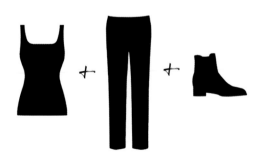

THE Vest

The vest is one of my all-time favorite personality pieces because of its amazing versatility! A vest adds a lively, refreshing element—like an exclamation point—to any silhouette outfit. Who knows, the signature vests I dressed Fran Drescher in for *The Nanny* may have won me the Emmy!

Vests come in a wide variety of fabrics and styles, offering so many cute and functional options for your casual wardrobe. Wear them under jackets, as outerwear, or as layering pieces. Go edgy with a leather motorcycle vest or athletic with a quilted equestrian style. Choose a long lace or crochet variety for a sweet, romantic vibe. Or borrow from men's fashion with a classic tailored suit-style vest. Whichever vest you choose, it's sure to add a special touch to your outfit.

THE Caftan

A lightweight sheer caftan adds a chic and exotic flair to your wardrobe. This long-sleeved, tunic-like garment has been worn for centuries in many cultures. Low-key and loose-fitting, a thigh-length, knee-length, or ankle-length caftan is the perfect garment for lounging around (in fact, it makes a lovely swimsuit cover-up). Ideal for warm weather, this garment is perfect to wear over straight-leg pants or jeans with a tank top and flat metallic sandals. Try wearing a sheer light cotton variety during the day and an embellished chiffon variety for fancier occasions, like a summer dinner party.

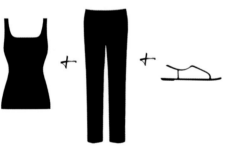

THE Denim Jacket

A denim jacket is an item every woman should have in her closet. Chic and hip, this casual piece offers a youthful vibe and can be worn with every silhouette combination and every style ID. To style, roll up the sleeves, flip up the collar, or add your favorite jewelry. Pair a structured dark denim jacket with a black pencil skirt and an ankle boot for a modern look you can also wear to work. For a more sophisticated look, wear it with a turtleneck, straight-leg black jeans, and a heeled ankle boot. Pull the look together with an elegant scarf.

THE
Duster

The duster is a loose-fitting type of coat or sweater coat that hits at or below the knee. Relaxed and always current, this ultraflattering gem pulls together any outfit and works beautifully for every body type, from petite to full-figured. Dress up a T-shirt and jeans or layer it over a pair of straight-leg pants and boots. Incredibly versatile, the duster adds a polished and modern finish to many looks. You can find dusters in luxurious modal blends, synthetic jersey, fluid cottons, and lightweight or heavyweight knits.

In cooler months, choose a heavier material or a knit fabric and pair it with an ankle boot. In warmer months, look for sheer or lightweight fabrics and add an exquisite heeled sandal. A duster is timeless, is perfect for travel, and can fit absolutely every style ID. My all-time favorite is a burgundy silk velvet duster I've worn for twenty years (and I intend to wear it for twenty more!).

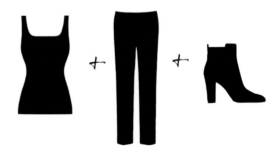

making the most of every moment

Creating an appealing casual wardrobe is a great way to add some inspiration to your closet. These eight style formulas will provide you with dozens of stylish outfits for the events of your everyday life—dates, happy hour, art openings, errands, dinner, and the gym. While you may not consider your free time to be a fashion priority (compared with what you wear to work), casual events are the places you network, build friendships, and make other exciting new connections.

When you dress in a way that is flattering, elegant, and appropriate, you will feel more confident, relaxed, and spontaneous in social situations. Clients have told me how they've made an important professional connection at a happy hour or found their significant other while running errands on the weekend. The right outfit has inspired them to seize the moment or take a risk—with rewarding results—all because they felt a greater sense of pride and excitement in their appearance.

With all you have to gain, why wouldn't you want to consistently dress in a way that makes you feel your best?

Remember that every moment is a chance to make your mark and step into your magnificence. Don't miss a single opportunity, darling! In the next chapter, we will talk about one of my favorite subjects: dressing up. I'm going to show you how easy and fun it can be to put together an outfit for a special occasion. I will give you the tools you need to walk into any event looking and feeling gorgeous! You will be amazed by how easy it is to use the Silhouette Solution to dress to the nines in a way that is stylish, comfortable, and totally you!

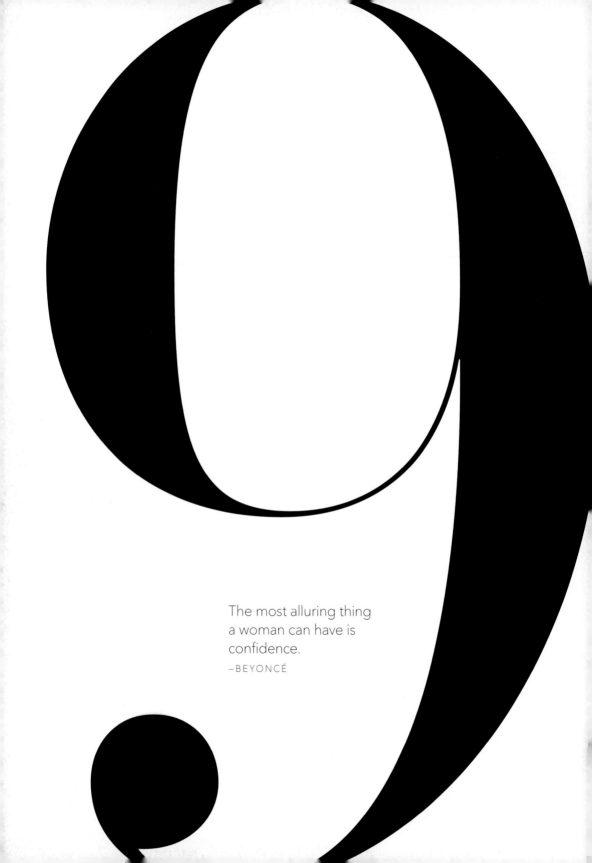

The most alluring thing
a woman can have is
confidence.
–BEYONCÉ

dressing for special occasions

PECIAL OCCASIONS DESERVE EXCEPTIONAL outfits. Whether you regularly attend black tie events or only get dressed up a few times a year, I'm sure that, like most women I know, you want to look amazing. The Silhouette Solution will help you accomplish that goal by assisting you in putting together show-stopping looks for extraordinary evenings.

The main difference between a dressy silhouette outfit and a casual one is the fabric. This is the time to trade in the cotton pencil skirt you wear for work and replace it with one made of a more glamorous material, such as my personal favorite, matte jersey knit. Sleek satin or sequins can also dress up an ensemble. Change your maxi skirt to a dressier mermaid shape or an elegant floor-length pencil skirt. Choose a palazzo pant in silk, charmeuse, or chiffon and an evening tank made of jersey knit, silk, charmeuse, velvet, or even sequins. Dressy silhouettes are also the perfect opportunity to bring out your heeled strappy sandal, your bejeweled flat sandal, or a black suede or satin stiletto ankle boot.

You may remember that I talked about wearing the silhouette necklines as a dress in chapter 3 ("The Perfect Length"). Whether turtleneck, tank, V-neck, scoop neck, or ultimate neckline, a dressy event is the perfect opportunity to wear that style

> A gorgeous pair of shoes will lift your spirits and your style. Make no mistake: Shoes are powerful.

in a knee-length or full-length dress or gown.

In these final eight formulas, I will show you how to put together elegant outfits for your dressiest occasions and special events, using the basic silhouette garments and chic, glamorous personality pieces.

There is no better place to start than with the garments you already have.

the great eight
for dressy occasions

Using the personality pieces highlighted in this chapter you can easily put together the perfect look for a wedding, charity gala, or night at the theater. We've all experienced the stress of trying to find "the perfect outfit." By employing the Silhouette Solution, you can use the clothes already in your closet to create a show-stopping look that makes you feel like a ten. Plus, you can avoid spending money on something you know you will only wear a few times.

Formula # 1

The
Ultimate Neckline

The
Maxi Skirt

The
Pump

THE Evening Wrap

A beautiful wrap adds sophistication to an evening ensemble while providing warmth. When there's a chill in the air, leave your coat at home and opt for a wrap instead. Allow it to hang loose over your forearms or throw an end over the opposite shoulder. Simple and traditional yet dramatic, this personality piece can be found in a variety of fabrics, such as heavy satin, silk, or velvet. Try a printed silk pashmina, a chiffon, or a fine cashmere to complete your look. Put on a magnificent pair of chandelier earrings, grab your purse, and you're ready to make an entrance.

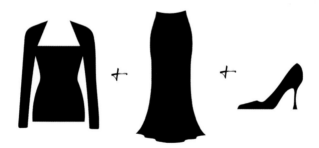

THE Statement Brooch

An eye-catching brooch or pin is a perfect way to express your style personality and add sparkle to a special outfit. From an exquisitely crafted vintage piece to a dazzling rhinestone number, a brooch shows off your creative side and is a great conversation piece. Brooches aren't just for the over-seventy set! Check out artisan shops to find unique styles, such as those crafted to look like dragonflies, cats, bumblebees, giraffes, and even flamingos. For those of you with an adventurous side, a brooch may become one of your go-to personality pieces.

A pin or brooch is traditionally placed on your lapel or near your shoulder, but feel free to play around with the placement to add a pop of color and individuality to your evening ensemble. I love my antique diamanté salamander and wear him regularly perched on the top of my left shoulder. You can also use your pins for casual outfits, adding some pizzazz to a denim jacket or the front of a purse.

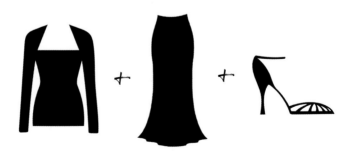

Formula # 2

The
Ultimate Neckline

The
Maxi Skirt

The
Strappy Sandal

Formula #3

The
Tank

The
Wide-Legged
Pant

The
Heeled
Ankle Boot

THE Glitzy Evening Jacket

A tailored jacket in velvet or embellished with sequins or bead-work adds instant glamour to an eveningwear ensemble. Bold and exciting, this jacket turns a simple silhouette outfit into a real eye-catcher. Perfect for holiday parties and weddings, you can find this personality piece in basic black or rich colors. The glitzy jacket pairs beautifully with the maxi skirt or the straight-leg pant. If all that sparkle just isn't you, opt for the simple lines and sheen of a black satin jacket. Add chandelier earrings and a beautiful evening purse, and you're ready for a festive night.

MONEY-SAVING TIP • Add this garment to your wardrobe around the first of the year, when holiday jackets go on clearance.

THE Statement Necklace

An easy way to dress up your outfit is to add a statement necklace. The beauty of this look is in its simplicity. Choose a top, a bottom, and a shoe, then add a statement necklace, and your dressy outfit is complete. I suggest choosing a necklace that sits on your upper chest if you're wearing the ultimate neckline so that it doesn't dip behind the fabric of your top. Faux gems, such as rhinestones, emeralds, rubies, sapphires, or black onyx are great choices for a statement piece.

Your necklace can be daring, whimsical, vintage, bohemian, or avant-garde—the choices are endless! My personal favorites are a gold-and-multicolored beaded beauty I found while exploring Little India in Los Angeles and my vintage 1960s rhinestone necklace that looks borrowed from Audrey Hepburn in *Breakfast at Tiffany's*.

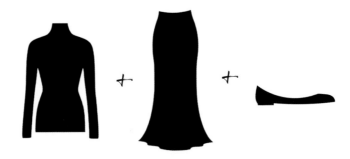

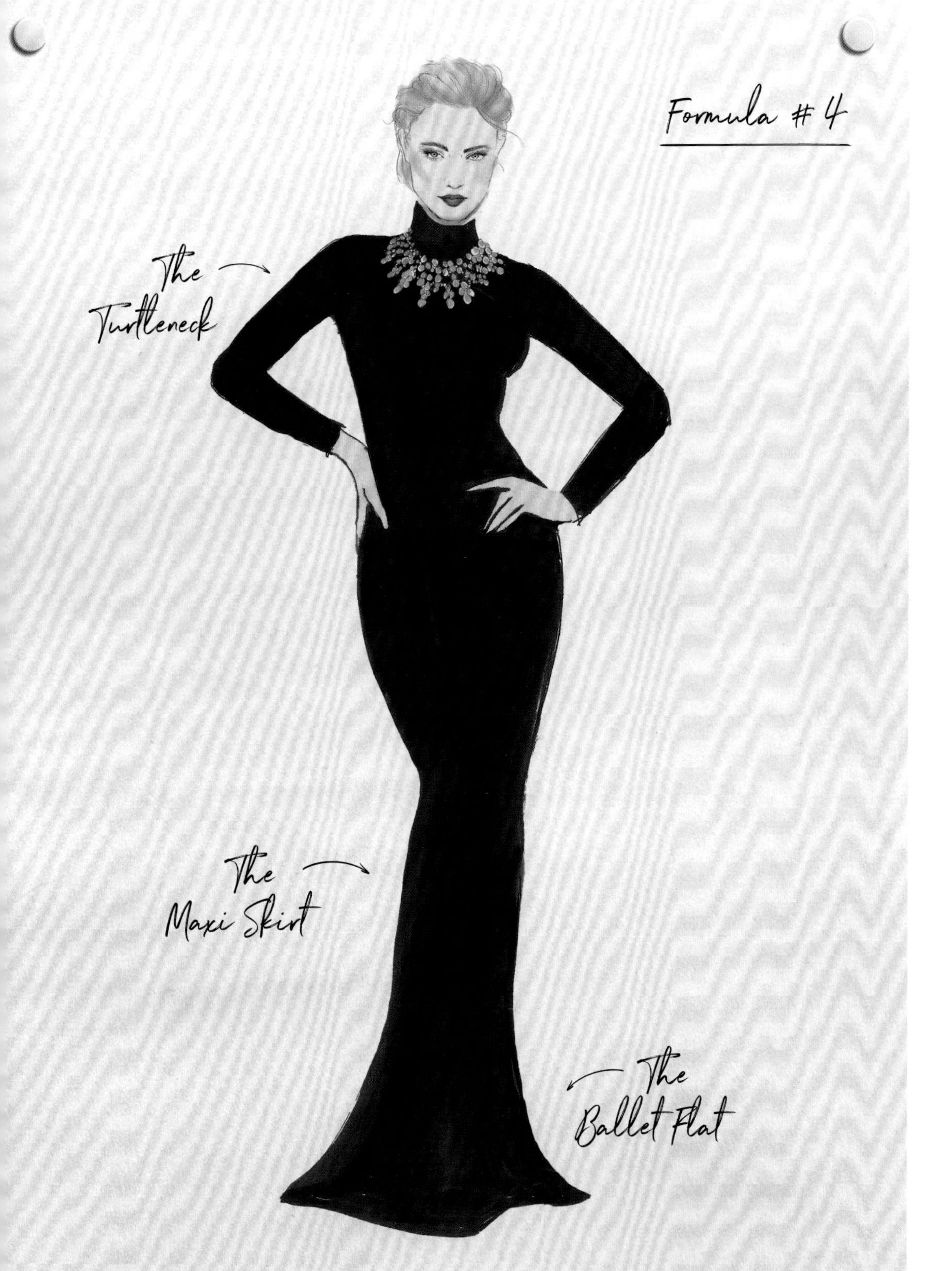

Formula # 4

The
Turtleneck

The
Maxi Skirt

The
Ballet Flat

Formula # 5

The
Tank

The Flounced
Pencil Skirt

The
Pump

THE Organza Blouse or Jacket

Organza has a delicate look and an airy feeling that makes an impression the moment it enters a room. Lightweight and sheer, with a subtle sheen similar to chiffon, organza appears stiffer and stands away from the body. This transparent fabric allows you to see the beautiful silhouette beneath. Available in pure silk or synthetic fabrics, it's the perfect personality piece for any special occasion outfit.

Look for a sheer evening swing coat or trench coat, a long-sleeved blouse, or a diaphanous wrap in black, champagne, teal, pink, or lilac. Organza pieces are timeless and elegant additions to your wardrobe.

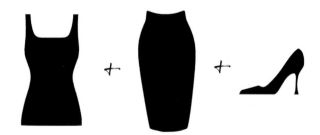

THE Shrug

The shrug is an essential personality piece for your special occasion wardrobe, but it works equally well for casual and work silhouettes. The ultimate shrug is a long-sleeved, open-front garment without closures that fits snugly on the upper body and ends just below the bust. Think of it as a cross between a bolero and a cropped cardigan. A shrug complements an outfit without overpowering it.

The shrug is also the perfect lightweight jacket for a chilly evening. You can find shrugs in elegant knits, chiffons, lace, or even velvet. If you are shy about your upper arms, the shrug allows you to wear sleeveless silhouette tops or strapless dresses with an option for coverage. This is an absolute staple in my wardrobe. More often than not, I don't leave home without one.

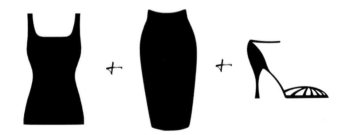

Formula # 6

The Tank

The Pencil Skirt

The Strappy Sandal

Formula # 7

The Ultimate
Neckline

The Evening
Palazzo Pant

The Heeled
Ankle Boot

THE Chandelier Earrings

Dating back to ancient Greece, these dangling beauties have a rich history. Set with suspended stones, chandelier earrings are not only on point for special occasions but can also dress up your favorite pair of jeans. You can count on them to complement the fluid fabrics of the silhouettes, balancing your face and elongating your neck. I enjoy knowing I can depend upon a pair of classic, glamorous, or bohemian chandelier earrings to provide me with an elegant touch for upscale events.

THE Evening Purse

When it comes to an evening purse, small and elegant is the way to go. You don't want a large leather shoulder bag or tote to steal the attention from your outfit. You need to carry only the essentials—such as your keys, ID, cell phone, and lipstick. Keep it simple with a glamorous clutch: a flat, envelope-style bag without a strap. My personal favorite is a small black-beaded clutch that rests comfortably in my hand. Evening purses come in an array of colors and styles, if you wish to make your purse a focal point. Choose one that steals the show!

Formula # 8

The Turtleneck

The Pencil Skirt

The Strappy Sandal

By investing in a few special occasion personality pieces and silhouettes, you'll have everything you need to look magnificent and feel confident. The best part is, you can be comfortable and glamorous at the same time—and what is more elegant than that? One of my go-to special occasion outfits is a black straight-leg pant, a matching tank, and a pair of matte black silk pumps. I finish my look with a stunning emerald green satin evening jacket and an evening clutch. I love how simple and relaxed a dressy look can be!

In the next chapter, we'll go shopping in your closet to begin building your Silhouette Solution wardrobe. There is no better place to start than with the garments you already have. Your closet likely has pieces we can use or reinvent. Using my simple method, I will help you sort out which garments to keep and which ones to retire. Let's get started!

Part three

It's
Transformation
Time

10

Happiness is making the most of
what you have; riches is making
the most of what you've got.
—ROSAMUNDE PILCHER

shopping your own closet

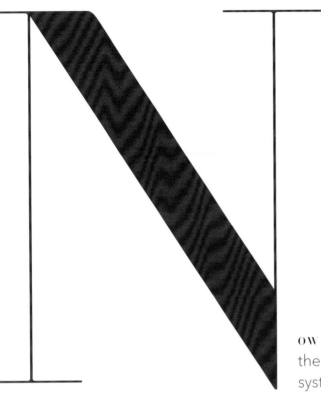

OW THAT YOU HAVE LEARNED ALL the pieces of the Silhouette Solution system and you have the 24 preset style formulas handy, it's time to revisit your closet. Using the same process I employ with my clients, we are going to build your own Silhouette Solution wardrobe, starting with the pieces you already have.

Joanne's Surprise Discovery

My client Joanne came to me wanting to redefine her image. She had some important functions coming up and wanted to look her best. My usual process in such cases is to offer a personal color consultation and a wardrobe edit, and then to go shopping. But Joanne wanted to jump from her color consultation directly to shopping.

She told me her closet was filled with junk—nothing we could use. I've heard this sentiment from clients on many occasions. From years of experience, I have learned that there are *always* garments that can be repurposed and reinvented as part of Silhouette Solution outfits. I talked Joanne into letting me do a 15-minute closet overview.

Four hours later, I emerged from her closet feeling very accomplished; Joanne was overjoyed. She had a completely new wardrobe without leaving her home or setting foot in a store. Joanne had beautiful pieces interspersed throughout her closet, and she didn't even know it. Using the Silhouette Solution system, we brought many of her personality pieces out of exile, and I coached her on how to use her existing garments to create modern, beautiful outfits.

Let's do the same for your closet! To begin, I'll have you identify all the daily activities and events for which you will be dressing (examples include your job, casual meetups, a night at the theater, and playdates). This will help you to know which pieces in your closet will be most useful to you and what to buy on future shopping trips.

Next, I'll help you identify which tops, bottoms, and shoes you already have so that you can start pulling together striking silhouette outfits. I'll also help you discover personality pieces you own now so that you can start building a complete, fabulous, and functional Silhouette Solution wardrobe.

In chapter 2, we visited your closet to observe and explore your current wardrobe and how the clothes in your closet made you feel. We looked at your emotional relationship with your clothes and the reasons you gravitate toward certain garments. If you skipped over that exercise, be sure to go back and complete it now (see page 47). This can give you valuable insight into your current clothing and help you build a wardrobe that increases your joy and confidence.

what do you dress for?

———

Your weekly activities and events may be many and diverse or few and simple. Or maybe you're transitioning into a new season. Perhaps you just got a new job, moved to a new city, or are transitioning from being a student to being a full-time employee. Whatever your circumstance, the Silhouette Solution can easily accommodate all of your dressing demands. The following exercise will help you evaluate your current wardrobe needs.

TRY IT! LIFESTYLE WARDROBE EVALUATION

1. Reflect on your style needs be it for work, casual, or dressy events. Grab a pencil.

2. In the work column, list all scenarios you encounter through the work that you do—whether virtual or in person—such as meetings, conferences, the PTA, client lunches, or interviews. Repeat the exercise, listing all casual occasions (a movie with friends, brunch, appointments) and dressy events (weddings, charity dinners, galas).

3. Review your list and reflect upon the activities you believe your wardrobe currently satisfies versus those for which you feel underprepared. For example, you may think that your work clothes are on point but struggle to know what to wear for an evening out with friends.

This list will save you time and help you make decisions as we look through your closet.

Work   Casual   Dressy

_____   _____   _____
_____   _____   _____
_____   _____   _____
_____   _____   _____
_____   _____   _____
_____   _____   _____
_____   _____   _____
_____   _____   _____
_____   _____   _____
_____   _____   _____
_____   _____   _____
_____   _____   _____
_____   _____   _____
_____   _____   _____
_____   _____   _____
_____   _____   _____
_____   _____   _____
_____   _____   _____
_____   _____   _____
_____   _____   _____
_____   _____   _____
_____   _____   _____

BUILDING THE SYSTEM
FROM YOUR CLOSET

Now that you have identified the activities you need to dress for, let's look in your closet and begin the transformation process! I've stepped into many different kinds of closets—some large and crammed full of clothes, others small and bare. In almost every space, I always find some foundational pieces to start building Silhouette Solution outfits.

Our first step will be to identify any silhouette tops, bottoms, or shoes you may have hiding in your closet. Begin by setting up your space. Clear an area in your room, such as your bed or a chair, where you can easily arrange your clothes. While you sort through your closet, reference the handy checklist on page 219. The checklist includes the 4 tops, 4 bottoms, 8 shoe styles that form your foundational silhouettes, and the 24 personality pieces you should search for in your closet. This will make is super easy for you to check off and see clearly what you already have and what's missing.

Ready to get started? Let's go!

1. Gather any of the four tops you find in your closet. Look for elongated or regular-length tank tops. Search for turtlenecks, plain T-shirts, or ultimate necklines (long, short, or sleeveless) in black, brown, navy, gray, or white. Also, pull out dresses in neutral colors that look like a tank, a turtleneck, a T-shirt, or an ultimate neckline.

2. Now, look for the four fab bottoms you own in black, brown, navy, gray, or white: straight-leg pants, wide-leg pants, maxi skirts, and pencil skirts. You may have a pair of dressy pants, jeans, or pull-on workout pants. If you don't have a pencil skirt or a maxi skirt, substitute an A-line or pleated skirt to start. Remember, our goal is to build an outfit that is the same color from top to bottom.

3. Next, find your Silhouette Solution shoes. Start by searching for ballet flats, flat sandals, flat ankle boots, and riding boots. Then add any heeled pumps, sandals, ankle boots, or knee-high boots you find. (Remember, we also discussed how to incorporate the smart loafer and the stylish sneaker into your silhouette outfits, so look for those, too.)

4. Set aside all potential pieces for foundational silhouette outfits. You may only have a few pieces, or you may discover you have more than you thought!

5. Now comes the fun part—finding your personality pieces. Start with work pieces: jackets (in any color), open-front drape cardigans, classic cardigans, trench coats, scarves, white button-up shirts, and blouses. Do the same for casual items, looking for denim and leather jackets, caftans, vests, and V-neck sweaters. For dressy pieces, pull out all of your shrugs, wraps, evening jackets, and clutches.

> In almost every space, I always find some foundational pieces to start building Silhouette Solution outfits.

I hope you will feel encouraged and inspired by what you found! Once you have pulled your potential silhouette pieces and personality pieces out of your closet, it's time to try them on and start to build some silhouette outfits.

During this part of the process, be honest with yourself. You need to evaluate if these garments fit and flatter your body. You are not looking at complete silhouette outfits yet; you are simply assessing individual elements.

Here are some dos and don'ts as you evaluate each garment:

- Do wear simple leggings or jeans when you try on tops.

- Do wear a tank top or sports bra when you try on bottoms.

- Do ask yourself the three questions about personality pieces (from chapter 6):

  – *Does the shape and style flatter my body?*

  – *Is the fabric fluid, and does it drape well on my body?*

  – *Does the color flatter my skin tone?*

- Do make sure each item fits. *Remember,* fit is as important as fashion! Wearing clothes that are a size (or multiple sizes) too small will never make you look smaller, and they often do the opposite. Also, identify items that are too big. If you find some ill-fitting pieces in your closet, retire them.

- Don't hang on to worn-out clothes. If a garment is threadbare, stretched out, stained, or has holes (that aren't part of the intended style), thank it for its service and toss it in the trash or bring it to a place that accepts textiles for recycling.

- Do retire outdated items. I'm not referring to your cool, vintage pieces, but I *am* talking about that bridesmaid dress that's been hanging in your closet for ten years. Throughout my life, I've said goodbye to countless pieces of clothing, and I always experience a sense of relief. You only make room in your closet for more pieces you truly love!

After you have tried on all your potential silhouette garments and personality pieces, set aside those you want to keep as part of your Silhouette Solution wardrobe. Whether you discovered five pieces or fifty, you have completed the first phase of reinventing your closet, your wardrobe, and yourself. Congratulations!

Remember, fit is as important as fashion!

have it / need it

This checklist will help you keep track of the Silhouette Solution garments you already have and those you want to add to your wardrobe. Simply place a check-mark on the pieces you have and leave the others blank. Feel free to make notes on what might need tailoring or replacing.

GARMENTS

4 TOPS, 4 BOTTOMS

- ◯ tank top
- ◯ turtleneck
- ◯ T-shirt
- ◯ ultimate neckline
- ◯ straight-leg pant
- ◯ wide-leg pant
- ◯ pencil skirt
- ◯ maxi skirt

SHOES

4 FLATS, 4 HEELS

- ◯ ballet flat (or smart loafer or stylish sneaker)
- ◯ flat sandal
- ◯ flat ankle boot
- ◯ riding boot
- ◯ pump
- ◯ heeled strappy sandal
- ◯ heeled ankle boot
- ◯ heeled knee boot

PERSONALITY PIECES

WORK

- ◯ black jacket
- ◯ colored jacket
- ◯ white shirt
- ◯ silk charmeuse blouse
- ◯ open-front drape cardigan
- ◯ classic cardigan
- ◯ perfect jewelry
- ◯ trench coat

PERSONALITY PIECES

CASUAL

- ◯ athletic jacket
- ◯ denim jacket
- ◯ leather jacket
- ◯ V-neck sweater
- ◯ vest
- ◯ caftan
- ◯ hoodie
- ◯ duster

PERSONALITY PIECES

DRESSY

- ◯ evening wrap
- ◯ statement brooch
- ◯ glitzy evening jacket
- ◯ statement necklace
- ◯ organza blouse or jacket
- ◯ shrug
- ◯ chandelier earrings
- ◯ evening purse

let's go shopping

Now that you've evaluated what you already have in your closet, I'll show you how to build your Silhouette Solution wardrobe from the ground up. You won't find every piece on one shopping trip, so don't even try. Whether you prefer to shop at department stores, at upscale boutiques, or online, I want to make your shopping experiences stress-free, fun, affordable, and empowering.

WHAT TO BUY FIRST

You may be wondering what items you should add to your Silhouette Solution wardrobe first. My advice is to start with the foundational silhouette pieces so you can build your first complete Silhouette Solution outfits.

TOPS

If you don't have one, start with a tank top, a versatile item you can use every day. The second piece I suggest purchasing is either the turtleneck or the T-shirt—depending on the climate you live in.

BOTTOMS

Your next purchase should be one of the bottoms. I'd start with either the straight-leg pant or straight-leg jean and a pencil skirt or maxi skirt. You'll get the most out of these versatile pieces, which are the building blocks of your silhouette outfits.

Pay attention to the silhouette pieces you naturally gravitate toward. My go-to pieces are the tank and either the straight-leg or wide-leg pants. On days that I want to create a more feminine look, I choose a maxi skirt. In colder months, I love the elegance of a turtleneck. Everyone's preferences will be different, and that's the beauty of this system. You don't have to use every piece, but each one is a tool you can use to look your best.

SHOES

If you are interested in buying one or more pairs of the eight great shoes, I would start with a black ballet flat and a flat metallic sandal (for warmer climates) or a flat ankle boot (for colder weather). Next, purchase a pair of pumps with a heel height you can comfortably walk in. If you can't wear heels, buy a cute wedge.

Collecting these basic items will give you the greatest number of outfit options right off the bat. You can certainly add to your wardrobe in any order you choose, but keep in mind that you are no longer just shopping mindlessly—you're now shopping with a purpose! Have fun and trust the process. You will soon have dozens of flattering possibilities.

Whether you prefer to shop at department stores, at upscale boutiques, or online, I want to make your shopping experiences stress-free, fun, affordable, and empowering.

how to buy on a budget

Every silhouette piece can be found at a variety of price points, from budget to designer. Some of my clients prefer to invest in more expensive foundational silhouette pieces, while saving the bargains for the personality pieces and accessories. Others would rather buy affordable silhouette pieces, leaving more of their budget available for personality pieces.

As I mentioned before, don't rush out and purchase your wardrobe all at once. You want to build your magnificent new closet and look over time, beginning with a few great outfits. I'm passionate about variety, so I purchase more affordable silhouette basics, allowing me to buy a greater number of personality pieces and accessories, but there's nothing wrong with investing in an expensive pair of pants or shoes that you plan to use again and again.

Your basic silhouettes won't change significantly from season to season. Designers will offer you the latest and greatest high-heeled pumps or straight-leg pants because it's their job to sell you clothes. But I haven't bought a pair of high-heeled pumps in years! I don't have to, because I have several gorgeous, timeless pairs that I adore and keep in tip-top shape. Remember, shoes can be repaired. Finding a good cobbler is a great investment in your style.

While the silhouettes stay the same through the years, personality pieces allow you to expand your wardrobe and accommodate different seasons. Your personality pieces also help you stay modern and stylish. Depending on your style ID (and your love for clothes and accessories), you'll probably have a greater number of personality pieces in your wardrobe than silhouette basics.

think like a stylist

Some people love to shop, and others loathe the experience. But having a purpose and knowing what you are shopping for can positively transform any shopping experience. My clients love how quickly and easily they can coordinate beautiful new outfits for any occasion at the mall, online, or in a boutique. I love to shop, but I meet many women who don't. Perhaps they've had bad experiences while shopping, don't like to spend money, have had a nightmare job working retail, or simply lack confidence to choose clothes they love. When I met Mary, she was such a woman.

CLIENT CONFESSIONS

Mary's New Attitude

When Mary came to me, she wanted to elevate both her professional appearance and her personal image, but she didn't know where to start. Shopping was one of her least favorite activities; it caused her stress and anxiety. She never knew which garments were right for her body type, and she lacked the confidence to make style decisions. For these reasons, the Silhouette Solution resonated with her. Once she understood the types of silhouette garments, shoes, and personality pieces to look for, she didn't feel as anxious about shopping.

I gave Mary tips on how to shop like a professional stylist, and I encouraged her to focus on fit over size, a factor that had discouraged her in the past. Two days later, I received an enthusiastic email from Mary. After our consultation, she immediately went shopping online and also went out and purchased several of the pieces in the system. She even bought garments she had never worn before, like the pencil skirt. She was thrilled with how she looked! She told me she had never expected to enjoy shopping, but with her new knowledge, she was excited to shop and add to her wardrobe.

how to shop like a pro

IN-STORE

1 **DRESS TO SHOP** • Nothing is more annoying than entering a dressing room and having to remove an entire outfit and shoes with laces. Wear a comfortable pull-on skirt or leggings and a T-shirt or tank top with slip-on shoes when you're going shopping.

2 **THINK ABOUT HAIR AND MAKEUP** • To get an accurate reading of how an outfit will look on you, wear your hair and makeup the way you normally would. Bring a ponytail holder to pull your hair back or up if needed. Sometimes an updo will give an outfit a whole new look.

3 **TRY IT ON** • The only way to know if clothes fit correctly and flatter your body is to try them on. Never take a garment home without trying it on. Save yourself the hassle of having to take something back to the store (or worse, having to absorb the cost of something you never wear). If you shop in a store, try it on then and there.

As you select garments to try on, don't concentrate on the numbers on the tags. Sizes often fit very differently from brand to brand, which can be frustrating and disheartening. Take a few sizes of each item into the dressing room and focus on how the garment fits and flatters *your* body. I've found beautiful clothes in the juniors department, in the maternity section (even when not pregnant), and in menswear! Don't let numbers define you.

4

BRING THE RIGHT UNDERGARMENTS AND SHOES • If you are shopping for an outfit that you know needs special under-garments, such as a strapless bra, bring them with you to try on with the garment. Similarly, if you have the shoes you plan to wear, bring them so you can check hem lengths. For example, when wearing high heels with dress pants, the hem should fall half an inch from the ground in the back.

5

LEAVE THE HEAVY TOTE AT HOME • Don't carry a heavy tote bag with you when you shop. You want to be as relaxed and unencumbered as possible. Use a lightweight crossbody bag to carry essentials so that your hands are free to pick up and touch garments.

These tips will help you have a relaxing, comfortable, and—I hope—*successful* shopping trip at your favorite clothing stores or boutiques.

ONLINE

1   **FIND THE RIGHT FIT** • Online shopping is a riskier way to buy clothes, because you can't try on garments before buying them. To help offset this risk, you can check sizing charts to find out if the clothes run true to size. One practice that has worked well for me is buying two different sizes of the same item and returning the one that doesn't fit. (Be sure to check the company's return policy first, as some stores make you pay shipping costs yourself to return items. In that case, you might be able to return the item to the brick-and-mortar store.)

2   **DO YOUR RESEARCH** • Many a sad online shopper has received an item that looked nothing like it did in the picture. Before you purchase something, read a detailed product description and identify the type of fabric. Checking out the customer reviews is also a great way to find out how clothes have fit others and if they've discovered issues with quality.

3   **UTILIZE ONLINE SEARCHES** • Every garment I've listed in this book can be typed into a search engine—for example, "soft leather jacket," "open-front cardigan," or "black palazzo pant." The internet is an excellent tool for researching different garments, fabrics, and colors, as well as gleaning inspiration for outfits that express your unique, personal style!

reinventing
your closet

Daunting as the task may seem, once you have identified the silhouette garments and personality pieces in your closet, you will no longer have to dig through the items you don't wear to get to those you do. As you continue to develop a stylist's discerning eye, you will become confident in making good decisions when you shop for items to complete your Silhouette Solution wardrobe.

With a little preparation and research, stocking your closet with the clothes you need for Silhouette Solution outfits can be fun and easy. Imagine going into a store and leaving with bags filled with beautiful, affordable garments that meet your lifestyle needs and express your individual style. It's possible! I've helped dozens of my clients do just that.

In the next chapter, we will complete the liberation of your closet. I'll show you how to organize your closet using four fabulous Silhouette Solution methods. Simply choose the one that best fits your personality and lifestyle. I have no doubt that your closet transformation will assist you in putting together beautiful outfits day after day, eradicating the "getting-dressed" blues, and making your morning routine a truly effortless and joyful experience!

> Imagine going into a store and leaving with bags filled with beautiful, affordable garments that meet your lifestyle needs and express your individual style. It's possible!

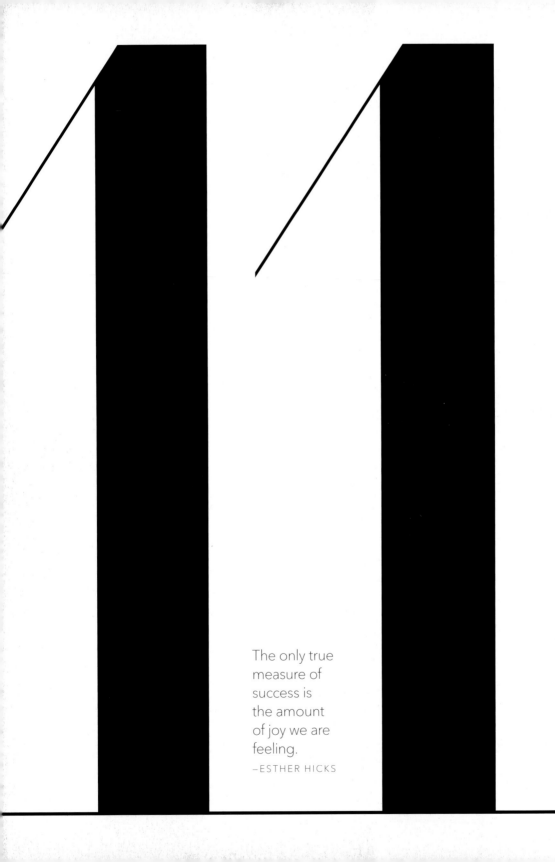

The only true
measure of
success is
the amount
of joy we are
feeling.
–ESTHER HICKS

set yourself up for success

WHEN WE BEGAN THIS STYLE adventure, we talked about the relationship you have with your clothes and how you feel about your closet. Your closet is a sacred space. It can either be a place of freedom, joy, and empowerment, or one of anxiety, frustration, and confusion. My goal in introducing you to the Silhouette Solution has been to totally transform how you feel when you enter your closet. I want you to feel inspired and empowered when choosing what to wear. Getting dressed truly can be one of the best parts of your day! That is just what my client Sally discovered when we took a deep dive into her closet.

I want
you to feel
inspired and
empowered
when choosing
what to wear.

Bright and vivacious, Sally was a creative director at an advertising agency. On the outside, she was always confident and enthusiastic but one look inside her closet revealed that she was "closet depressed"—her closet was an overwhelming mess of disorganized garments, accessories, and shoes. Sally admitted that on most mornings, a wave of anxiety washed over her when she thought about walking into her closet to get dressed.

Her usual morning routine involved a chaotic half hour of trying on various outfits and rejecting each one because she didn't like how it looked. By the end of the week, all these outfits would morph into a giant pile on the floor and grow larger until she had time to tackle the arduous task of organizing them.

While the Silhouette Solution was a welcome way to streamline her busy life, in order to reap the full benefits of the system, Sally needed to set up her closet according to one of my four favorite organization methods. A tidy closet allowed Sally to easily see and select her silhouettes and personality pieces. Instead of digging through a pile of clothes on the floor or flipping through a wall of clothes hanging in the closet, she could easily access (and assess) all her options at once. Having worked in so many different types of closets and with so many satisfied clients, I told her that she could expect to feel less stressed and more inspired in an organized space.

liberate your closet

———

Preparing your closet to best utilize the Silhouette Solution will greatly enhance your experience with the system. I've taught you how to make the Silhouette Solution work on your body; now it's time to make it work inside your closet. This process can be both fun and freeing!

When I walk into my closet, every item has a function and a purpose. I can see exactly which garments I have to choose from. I don't have to sort through clothes I never wear to get to the ones I do. Instead, I see only garments I love that make me feel beautiful. Let's go through your closet and do the same for you!

TOOLS FOR SUCCESS

My philosophy is that a woman should treat her closet as a room unto itself. Having the right tools to organize will add to the enjoyment of your clothes. Here are a few tips.

- Use the same style of hangers throughout your wardrobe. Using matching hangers allows clothes to hang at a uniform height and in the same shape. It can also save space. The simple act of unifying your hangers will create a more harmonious and visually pleasing environment. My personal favorites are slim black velvet, nonslip hangers that take up minimal space and bring a classy calmness to my closet.

- I recommend going online to purchase some round clothing rack dividers. These will help you divide various sections of your closet. Label them "tops," "bottoms," "personality: work," "personality: casual," "personality: dressy," or using any categories that help you quickly access your options.

- Buy some sheer white organza gift pouches with a drawstring ribbon closure to hang jewelry or smaller accessories in your closet. You can hang these pretty pouches on the same hanger as your outfit or on a door organizer.

- Invest in a belt hanger and a scarf hanger. I prefer the types that hang on the closet rail, but you can find many styles online.

- Use a shoe rack or place shoes in a spot where they can stay on display. Organize shoes by color and type (such as boots, pumps, ballet flats, sandals).

four ways to organize your closet

I have taught many clients how to reinvent and reorganize their closets for maximum efficiency using the Silhouette Solution. While doing this requires some up-front time and effort, once you've set up your closet, I guarantee you will love it (and love getting dressed)!

Simply choose one of these four organizational methods to easily coordinate stunning silhouette outfits.

1

ORGANIZE BY FUNCTION

If you regularly engage in two or more spheres that require different wardrobes—for example, work and casual events—organizing by function may be the way to go. Perhaps you wear suits and structured clothing on weekdays but love expressing your bohemian style on the weekends. Or maybe you get dressed up several nights a week. If this system appeals to you, follow the steps to organize your wardrobe by function.

1. Think about the outfits you wear on a weekly basis. You can refer to the Work/Casual/Dressy list you made on page 215.

2. Gather all the pieces you wear for work—pants, skirts, jackets, coats, cardigans, blouses—and set them aside. Do the same with casual clothing and dressy attire. You may also want designated piles for other standard outfits you wear, such as gym clothes, hiking attire, or work uniforms.

3. Divide your closet into three main areas: work, casual, and dressy. For simplicity, you may want to keep it at three, but you also may want to subdivide each of the sections—such as date night, travel, and gym—according to your lifestyle needs.

4. Hang all of your work clothes, including personality pieces and silhouette pieces, in your work section. Place your foundational silhouette tops and bottoms at the front of each section—these will be the pieces you reach for first. Don't worry if you don't have them all right now; you will gather them over time. Next, hang personality pieces according to type. For example, hang all work jackets together, all cardigans next to one another, and all blouses in a row.

5. Go through the same process for your casual area, your dressy area, and any other sections you have created. Place a round rack divider between sections.

WHY IT WORKS • With this system, the garments you need to dress for recurring occasions are always at your fingertips.

2

ORGANIZE BY GARMENT

Use this organizing system if you want to keep similar garments together: pants with pants, skirts with skirts, and jackets with jackets. If you find that many of your garments cross over between occasions, this way of organizing may be for you. You will divide your closet into two sections: silhouettes and personality pieces.

1. Empty your closet, placing all garments on your bed or on another available space. Separate your clothes into two categories: silhouette pieces (the four tops and four bottoms) and personality pieces (as described in chapters 6 to 9).

2. Place each silhouette piece on a separate hanger. You may not have all of these pieces right now, but here is the hanging order I suggest: Hang straight-leg pants first, followed by wide-leg pants to the right. Next, continuing from left to right, hang your pencil skirts and then your maxi skirts. You can hang them to the right or the left, depending upon your preference. For the tops, hang your tanks, followed by your T-shirts, your turtlenecks, and, finally, your ultimate necklines.

   Hang all silhouette pieces in the same section of your closet. Remember to always wear the same color on top and bottom. Never mix and match silhouette colors! So, place all black silhouettes together, all navy silhouettes in proximity, and all brown silhouettes near one another, ending with your white or light-colored warm weather silhouettes. Silhouette pieces should take up a small area of your closet, leaving more space for personality pieces.

3. Hang your personality pieces in their own area, according to garment type. Hang jackets together, shirts next to one another, cardigans in a group, and so on.

WHY IT WORKS • This system allows you to quickly assemble an outfit based on the specific garments you feel like wearing.

3

ORGANIZE BY OUTFIT

If you are one of those women who stares into their closet for what seems like hours, stressing over how to assemble the perfect outfit, this system is for you. Imagine having beautiful, pre-styled outfits waiting for you just inside your closet door! No more frantic searching through your closet, trying to coordinate an attractive outfit in a rush. This system focuses on coordinating complete, ready-to-wear outfits ahead of time.

1. Choose an area with good lighting (preferably natural light) and use a full-length mirror or the closest thing you have to it. You may want to use your phone or a camera to take pictures of some of your outfits for future reference. If possible, bring in a friend whose opinion you trust to help vet your outfit choices.

2. Begin with work outfits. Choose a pair of silhouette pants or a skirt as your anchor piece. Add a matching silhouette top. If you can pull together a complete silhouette outfit by adding shoes, even better. Now, add personality pieces, such as a white shirt, a cardigan, jewelry, and a purse. Coordinate elements until you have a polished and styled look. Take a picture!

3. Try a different look with that same silhouette bottom. Try flats, heels, or boots, and add a jacket or scarf. Be sure to use some of the lesser-worn personality pieces you own. You may be surprised to discover new alternatives and great outfits within your existing closet. Keep going until you feel like you've run out of all the looks you could possibly create with that one skirt or pants. Try to pull together at least five different looks for work.

4. Using the same method, coordinate at least five different ensembles for your casual days. Start with straight-leg jeans paired with one of the four tops. Then pull together a complete outfit that includes personality pieces and accessories.

5. Next, coordinate one or two dressy outfits that you could wear for a special occasion. Remember to choose rich fabrics with sheen or even sparkle. Then add dressy details, such as gemstone earrings, high heels, and a glamorous wrap.

6. When you've finished, look back through your photos. Select the outfits that make you look and feel most attractive and confident. Place your photos in an online file or, if you want to go old school, you can print them out and create a photo album (what we in the fashion industry call a "lookbook").

7. After you've created your lookbook, hang your outfits as you've created them in your closet. Use one or two hangers for each outfit. For jewelry, I use white organza fabric storage pouches, looped over the hanger. Keep your shoes on display for easy visual access.

Next time you're in a rush to get out the door, imagine having a stylish silhouette outfit ready to go! This system does take some dedication and planning in advance, but it also allows you to build your wardrobe intentionally by filling in the garments you need to complete stellar outfits. I recommend going through this process once every few months to keep it maintained and create new outfits as needed. As you become familiar with the technique, it will become quicker, and more creative and fun.

WHY IT WORKS • This method provides stylish, ready-to-go silhouette outfits and eliminates the guesswork of getting dressed each morning.

4

ORGANIZE BY COLOR

Organizing by color is great for creative, outside-the-box thinkers, and closets organized this way are a sight to behold! When I visited Rio de Janeiro, I was stunned the first time I walked into a clothing store. The shops arrange their garments by color! The rainbow effect of the reds, oranges, yellows, greens, purples, and blues grouped together was breathtaking! If you wake up each day thinking, "What color should I wear today?" this system is for you!

1. On your bed or another available space, arrange all of your clothes in piles by color. For example, place all blue garments—both silhouette pieces and personality pieces—in a single pile. Do the same with reds, yellows, greens, and blues, in addition to neutral colors, like black, gray, white, and beige.

2. Place your garments on hangers and hang them in your closet by color. Hang all garments of a single color together in one section. Place similar items of each color, such as jackets or pants, in their own smaller groupings. I suggest organizing from your darkest colors (black, brown, navy, and gray) to your vibrant rainbow colors—red, orange, yellow, green, blue, and violet. Within each individual color section, organize from dark to light.

3. Using organza pouches, hang accessories and jewelry by color within each section.

4. Consider how different colors can inspire different moods and the image certain colors portray (see page 240).

A closet organized by color is a closet where you will feel inspired to get dressed each morning. Adding color to your wardrobe adds energy to your life!

WHY IT WORKS • This system allows you to harness the power of color and create excitement in your wardrobe and in your life.

WHAT DOES COLOR SAY ABOUT YOU?

To feel **confident** and **assertive**, wear

red.

To appear **soft** and **approachable**, wear

pink.

To **stand out** in a crowd, wear

yellow.

To appear **edgy** and nontraditional, wear

orange.

To feel **calm** and **centered**, wear

blue.

To appear **elegant** and **sophisticated**, wear

black.

To look **sophisticated** but with a **softer edge**, wear

brown or

navy.

To appear **spontaneous** and **fun**, wear

turquoise.

taking action

———

Remember Sally? Because color is an important part of her creative work as an advertising executive, Sally decided to organize her garments by color. Today, a space that once inspired feelings of anxiety now inspires serenity and joy. Instead of dropping her clothes on the floor at the end of the day, she hangs them up in their designated areas. Thanks to Sally's organized space, she is able to create modern, elegant Silhouette Solution outfits quickly and easily every day!

If you battle with a cluttered closet (as so many of us do), I encourage you to push through and see for yourself how an organized closet can bring you a sense of joy and control. Once you have chosen the closet organization method that works best with your personality and lifestyle, set aside an afternoon to overhaul your closet. You will be amazed at how your outer closet and inner closet are connected. An organized outer closet calms and soothes the inner closet of our limiting beliefs, opening up space for greater creativity and positivity. Once you take the plunge and organize your space, you will feel a fresh, new energy putting together outfits. Even better, you will leave your closet feeling stylish, confident, and in control.

> Once you take the plunge and organize your space, you will feel a fresh, new energy putting together outfits. Even better, you will leave your closet feeling stylish, confident, and in control.

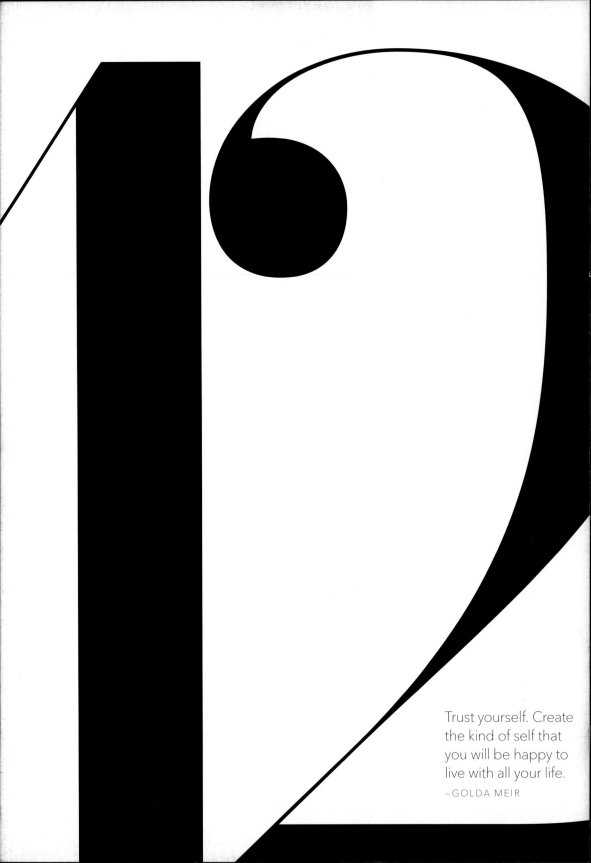

12

Trust yourself. Create
the kind of self that
you will be happy to
live with all your life.
—GOLDA MEIR

your
time to
shine

UR STYLE ADVENTURE TOGETHER IS nearing its end, but what lies ahead is a new beginning and the opportunity for you to make your next act your best one ever! I celebrate you for staying on board, and I hope you feel inspired by what you have learned along the way. My purpose and passion of informing and empowering women has only grown during my thirty-year career as a designer and stylist. I've had the privilege of helping many women identify the negative, defeating thoughts lurking in their "inner closets" and transforming them into empowering messages of self-approval and self-acceptance.

CLIENT CONFESSIONS

Treya's True Style

Treya is a communication course leader for a large organization. One day, I was tasked with revamping her appearance for an important seminar she would be delivering the following morning. Treya was not thrilled with the idea of going shopping; she was comfortable with her look and wasn't very excited about changing up her clothing choices. However, she decided to trust me.

Treya had experienced a challenging childhood that included abuse. As a result, her approach to dressing was based on hiding her body and herself. This was ironic, considering that her job (which she was great at) required her to speak in front of large groups. Even though she had a petite frame, she wore long sleeves, high necklines, voluminous scarves, and oversize clothing.

We had a quick chat before heading out on our shopping excursion. I explained my style philosophy and asked some questions. I discovered that Treya preferred classic, traditional clothes styled in nontraditional ways. She liked to feel modern and youthful without much embellishment. Her style ID was a combination of the minimalist and the conservative, to which she added her own unconventional twist.

Despite her initial apprehension, Treya's attitude quickly changed as we began to select outfits that showcased her beauty and personality. I dressed her in a tailored, navy knee-length pencil skirt with a fitted high-neck tank. Over this sleek silhouette, I added an elegant, elongated single-breasted blazer with a structured shoulder line. A pair of navy suede block-heeled pumps completed the ensemble.

Treya looked powerful, feminine, and modern—and she knew it! The moment she looked in the mirror, a huge smile spread across her face. "Now I get it!" she said. Treya had never imagined she could feel comfortable and confident in clothing that was formfitting. She left the store with not just one outfit but a dozen garments she could mix and match to create a whole new professional wardrobe that was easily adaptable for casual and even dressy events.

Treya was thrilled that we could achieve this in one afternoon. "When you know what you're looking for, it's easy!" I told her. She was both astonished and delighted to discover that wearing truly flattering clothes all but eliminated her desire to hide. She told me she felt a new freedom, ease, and comfort with her appearance that she had never felt as an adult. The next day, Treya led her seminar with the confidence you get from knowing you look great.

Now it's your turn to step into the best version of yourself. Using the Silhouette Solution, you can experiment with your style and have fun. You deserve to look and feel fabulous every day of your life, and by using the tools in this book, you're equipped to discover your own individual beauty and style. When you believe in yourself and dress in a way that is authentically you, you will be amazed to see how your inner and outer life transform!

We all deserve to feel comfortable and vibrant every day, regardless of our age, size, or shape. And possessing a versatile wardrobe filled with flattering clothes you love will surely boost your confidence to be your best self. Now, getting dressed and looking attractive will be quick and effortless, because your wardrobe will be stocked with the garments you need for every season and occasion. You'll spend less time in your closet and more time focusing on what is important to you. Shopping will be a breeze, because now you know exactly what to buy, and you don't have to break the bank by keeping up with the ever-changing trends.

How do I know? I've seen it happen again and again for my clients. Treya is a perfect example (page 245).

I want every woman to feel the way Treya did that day. You do not have to have the perfect body to wear the garments of the Silhouette Solution.

(And what is "perfect," anyway?) You do not have to be a certain size. You don't have to be a fashionista. The system works for anybody! All you have to do is be *willing* to start, right where you are.

Whatever your current situation, you deserve to feel confident today. You don't have to lose weight, do more crunches, or go down a size to look amazing. You already *are* amazing, darling! Giving yourself the green light to be yourself and step into your magnificence takes courage. Leaving old ways (and old clothes) behind may feel unfamiliar at first, but as you let go of the habits and negative ways of thinking that you may have clung to in the past, you will find a more empowered, confident version of you.

I encourage you to use the Silhouette Solution to reframe how you relate to yourself—and your clothes—in an empowering new way. This might feel foreign at first, but in the end, it will be tremendously fulfilling.

While some people may believe that fashion and image are superficial, I disagree. When you look your best, you *feel* your best. And when you feel your best, you *do* your best. When we look and feel confident, we are more willing to take risks and go outside our comfort zone. I have watched clients put themselves out there in ways they previously would have avoided, because they suddenly feel attractive and powerful. Taking those risks can produce wonderful rewards, including feelings of fulfillment and accomplishment.

Look in the mirror and celebrate the amazing and unique person looking back at you. You are fabulous! And there is only one you. My hope is that you use the Silhouette Solution to revitalize your closet and revolutionize your confidence. No matter who you are, you *can* look amazing in every area of your life!

As you integrate the Silhouette Solution system into your life, acknowledge your strengths and give yourself permission to go after what you want from life. And don't let the transformation stop with you! Pass on a legacy of confidence and self-acceptance to your loved ones, friends, and children. Think of this system of dressing as your first step toward fulfilling your goals and dreams. When we dress for the life we want, we are more alert to the many opportunities available to help us step into a more meaningful existence.

Nothing would give me greater joy than for you to use this book as an ongoing resource of empowerment and inspiration. Now it's *your* time to shine.

When we dress for the life we want, we are more alert to the many opportunities available to help us step into a more meaningful existence.

RESOURCES

THE INNER CLOSET CHECKLIST TO FEELING YOUR BEST

THINGS TO CULTIVATE

Self-acceptance
Self-acknowledgment
Self-forgiveness
Self-gratitude
Self-love
Compassion
Inner joy
Being authentic

THINGS TO UPROOT

Comparisons to others
Self-judgment
Body shame
Limiting beliefs
Disempowering
"Should haves"
The chase of perfection
Negative self-talk

A GUIDE TO SHAPEWEAR SUCCESS

The right shapewear can help you feel more confident. It can be a wonderful tool when wearing a special occasion dress or even for an everyday confidence booster. The purpose of shapewear is to minimize some curves and enhance others: "to rearrange the real estate." If you want to give shapewear a try but don't know where to start, any of the following three shapers are attractive and get the job done.

FULL-BODY SLIMMER • This full-body slip or body suit with a built-in bra provides full coverage so that your overall appearance is smoother.

HIGH-WAIST THIGH SHAPER • These bicycle-style shorts smooth the thighs, create an hourglass look, support the rear, and pull in the tummy.

HIGH-WAIST HALF-SLIP SHAPER • This piece does not contain a built-in bra but covers the stomach, hips, and thighs. It creates a smooth surface for your skirt or dress to slip over. It smooths the thighs, pulls in the tummy, and eliminates a "muffin top."

SHAPEWEAR CHECKLIST

Make sure your shapewear fits correctly so you're not in for a day of discomfort and irritation. Here's my checklist to ensure the most comfortable fit.

COMPLETE SMOOTHING • The shapewear's purpose is to smooth your body completely. If your shapewear is not laying effortlessly, try a different size.

NO ROLLING • Move around in your shapewear to make sure it does not roll up at the waist, leg, or hem.

NO PEEKING • Make sure the shapewear is not visible under your garment, especially when you sit down.

NO-BUDGE WAIST • The waist of the shaper should stay in place when you move around. Be sure to walk around and try sitting and standing to make sure the shaper doesn't slip down.

NON-BINDING LEGS • When wearing a shaper with shorts, be sure it does not cut into your leg, which can be bad for your circulation and create a bulge that can be visible under pants and skirts.

COMFY CROTCH • Make sure the crotch of your shapewear does not hang too low or ride too high, which will make you uncomfortable. Pull it on just like you would a pair of jeans and make sure the crotch is properly positioned as an undergarment would be.

NO DOWNSIZING • Warning, going down a size in shapewear will not make you look smaller! Instead, you will look bigger. Shapewear comes in different control levels: light, moderate, firm, and extra firm. Choose your regular size in the shapewear and increase the control level for a slimmer look.

THE SILHOUETTE SOLUTION
FIRST-AID KIT

––––––––––

When it comes to clothing, stuff happens! Fabric tears, buttons pop off. I expect such mishaps and always carry a fashion emergency tool kit to solve these problems on the spot. Put together your own kit to keep in your bag or take along on trips.

SAFETY PINS • Helpful for many fashion emergencies, safety pins can fix a dropped hem, adjust an errant neckline, or even stand in for a missing button. I carry the small black variety for dark clothes and small silver or white ones for lighter colored clothing.

BLACK SHARPIE • This little gem is great for covering scuff marks on black shoes or bleach spots on dark garments.

TRAVEL LINT ROLLER • A mini lint brush is great to have on the go for removing hair, fluff, or debris that may have gathered on your garment.

QUICK-FIX SEWING KIT • A tiny sewing kit that contains pre-threaded needles can be found at hotels and in drug stores. Use them to repair split seams, loose buttons, or dropped hems.

FASHION TAPE • This clear double-sided tape in individual strips is an old Hollywood trick. It's a fast solution for when a pant, skirt, or jacket hem drops. It also comes in handy when a belt is too long and flopping or a blouse falls too far away from the body, exposing your bra. This tape attaches the fabric to the skin with no irritation.

DISPOSABLE UNDERARM PADS • These peel-and-stick sweat pads are made to keep perspiration from leaving a mark on the interior of a blazer or blouse.

PORTABLE MINI STEAMER • I highly recommend this item for your travels. A steamer quickly removes creases from clothing while it's still on the hanger (and is easier to use than hauling out the hotel iron).

HAIRSPRAY • Not only can hairspray be helpful in freshening up your locks, it can also remove makeup marks on collars of shirts or blouses. Spray directly on a stain and buff gently with a soft cloth (test on the fabric first in an inconspicuous spot).

BABY WIPES • These multipurpose wonders aren't just for diaper bags. They are great for eliminating stains, cleaning up spills, removing makeup, and generally freshening up. I always carry a portable pack in my bag.

SMALL SCISSORS • A pair of small scissors is always good to have on hand to cut any loose threads or remove tags.

SHOE MAINTENANCE LIST

Did you know that your shoes are the first thing others subconsciously notice about you? Keep yours looking great (and your feet feeling great) with this list of tips and tricks.

POLISH • Make sure your shoes always look their best: Eliminate scuff marks by polishing your shoes if they are leather and using a soft brush to remove any dirt if they are suede.

STRETCH • If your shoes feel too tight, fill a misting spray bottle with water, spray the inside of the shoes, and wear them wet for a couple of hours to stretch them out.

SCORE • Don't want to slip in your new shoes? Use a box cutter knife or sharp blade to score the soles of your shoes in a crisscross pattern. This will create more grip and traction when you walk.

MINIMIZE NOISE • Are your shoes noisy? Hard floors and heels can raise quite the ruckus! One option is to have your local shoe repair shop add a thin layer of charcoal-colored dance rubber to the sole of your shoe or boot to quiet your step and prolong the life of the shoes.

CREATE COMFORT • If shoes are pinching in particular areas or causing blisters, apply a piece of soft moleskin to the uncomfortable area of the shoe (not to your foot) to ease the discomfort.

EVALUATE • Be on the lookout for signs of wear and tear on your shoes and replace them as necessary. Worn-down heels, broken heel cups, worn-out soles, and a stained or shabby appearance are all signs you may need new shoes.

SHOPPING LIST

THE SILHOUETTE PIECES

- ○ Tank
- ○ Turtleneck
- ○ T-Shirt
- ○ Ultimate Neckline
- ○ Straight-Leg Pant (or jeans or leggings)
- ○ Wide-Leg Pant
- ○ Maxi Skirt
- ○ Pencil Skirt
- ○ Flat Sandal
- ○ Ballet Flat (or sneakers or loafers)
- ○ Flat Ankle Boot
- ○ Riding Boot
- ○ Pump
- ○ Heeled Strappy Sandal
- ○ Heeled Ankle Boot
- ○ Heeled Knee Boot

SHOPPING LIST

THE PERSONALITY PIECES

- ○ Black Blazer
- ○ Colored Jacket
- ○ White Shirt
- ○ Silk Charmeuse Blouse
- ○ Open-Front Drape Cardigan
- ○ Classic Cardigan
- ○ Perfect Jewelry
- ○ Trench Coat
- ○ Athletic Jacket
- ○ Denim Jacket
- ○ Leather Jacket
- ○ V-Neck Sweater
- ○ Vest
- ○ Caftan
- ○ Hoodie
- ○ Duster
- ○ Wrap
- ○ Statement Brooch
- ○ Glitzy Jacket
- ○ Statement Necklace
- ○ Organza Jacket
- ○ Shrug
- ○ Chandelier Earrings
- ○ Statement Purse

ACKNOWLEDGMENTS

The next time you purchase a new piece of clothing, take a moment to reflect upon the extraordinary number of people who contributed to the creation of your new garment. From the farmers, fabric weavers, pattern cutters, and sewers, to the dyers, buyers, and even the salesperson who may have sold you your garment—so many people played a part.

It's the same for a book. My dream of becoming an author would never have been possible without the support, extraordinary expertise, and collaboration of a group of brilliant minds. The result is the book you are holding right now. I am so grateful, appreciative, proud, and indebted to this team—and I am utterly delighted to acknowledge them.

To my dear friend and soul sister Marina Barone, for your unwavering friendship and emotional support. I am so grateful to you for your huge contribution and always being there by my side from inception to completion on this transformative journey. You are the best thinking partner a girl could ever ask for. I love you.

Thank you to my literary agent, Cassie Hanjian, for your awesome guidance, attention to detail, and coaching through the proposal and manuscript process. Thanks also to Caryn Karmatz Rudy, for so brilliantly taking over where Cassie left off. Thank you for your attentiveness and guidance—always listening to my thoughts and ideas with such patience, grace, and kindness.

To Suzanne Gosselin. What a delightful partnership. How you culled and edited 75,000 words with such freedom and ease I will never know—always with a smile on your face and while being a mom to four beautiful, energetic young children.

To my friend Kathy Ver Eecke, for inviting me to join your writing workshop that led to the introduction to my agent Cassie, which in turn led to my dream, a book deal. I love how the pieces of the puzzle of life and a dream come together.

Thank you to my friend Professor Lorrie Ivas, for letting me sit in your fashion research library and flip through scores of vintage issues of *Vogue* and *Harper's Bazaar* for design inspiration. And to Chris Brempel and Randy Bruck, for your graphic design expertise on the icons. And Professor Jemi Armstrong, for being a wealth of knowledge and resource for everything "fashion."

To Amanda Englander, for seeing my vision and bringing me to Clarkson Potter, and to Angelin Borsics, my editor, for leading the charge in shaping all the elements into a book that I am so, so proud of. To Jan Derevjanik, who deftly translated my vision into a gorgeous design. To my brilliant production editor, Terry Deal, and expert copy editor, Amelia Ayrelan Iuvino, for polishing my language and prose. And lastly, to Kim Tyner, whose perfect color proofing and production work resulted in the most gorgeous book that I'm proud to share. You guys rock!

Finally, a very special thank-you to a bold, beautiful, brilliant woman and friend: Fran Drescher. You have been a contribution to others for decades and exemplify what it means to "live out loud" with passion, purpose, and humor. May you continue to be an example to us all! Thank you for recognizing my talent and choosing me to be your designer on *The Nanny* (the most fun job I've ever had!). Your generous acknowledgment and support of my purpose, passion, and talent means the world to me.

Published in the United States by Clarkson Potter/
Publishers, an imprint of Random House, a division
of Penguin Random House LLC, New York.
clarksonpotter.com

CLARKSON POTTER is a trademark and POTTER
with colophon is a registered trademark of Penguin
Random House LLC.

Library of Congress Cataloging-in-Publication Data
Names: Cooper, Brenda (Fashion designer), author.
Title: The silhouette solution : using what you
have to get the look you want / Brenda Cooper ;
illustrations by Jessica Durrant.
Identifiers: LCCN 2020056187 (print) | LCCN
2020056188 (ebook) | ISBN 9780593139103
(paperback) | ISBN 9780593139110 (ebook)
Subjects: LCSH: Clothing and dress. | Fashion. |
Women's clothing.
Classification: LCC TT507 .C6625 2021 (print) | LCC
TT507 (ebook) | DDC
 746.9/2–dc23
LC record available at https://lccn.loc.
gov/2020056187
LC ebook record available at https://lccn.loc.
gov/2020056188

ISBN 978-0-593-13910-3
Ebook ISBN 978-0-593-13911-0

Printed in China

Editor: Angelin Borsics
Manuscript Editor: Suzanne Gosselin
Designer: Jan Derevjanik
Illustrator: Jessica Durrant
Production Editor: Terry Deal
Production Manager: Kim Tyner
Compositors: Merri Ann Morrell and Nick Patton
Copy Editor: Amelia Ayrelan Iuvino

10 9 8 7 6 5 4 3 2 1

First Edition